M U R D E R

IN CARLISLE'S EAST END

....

UNINTENDED CONSEQUENCES

FOREWORD BY DAVID L. SMITH

PAUL D. HOCH

Charleston · London

THE
History
PRESS

Published by The History Press
Charleston, SC 29403
www.historypress.net

Copyright © 2014 by Paul D. Hoch
All rights reserved

First published 2014

Manufactured in the United States

ISBN 978.1.62619.515.8

Library of Congress CIP data applied for.

To Georgia Corvino for sharing such intimate and vivid details of her life and for being the inspiration that reminds us of the strength of the human spirit and the depth of character that allow us to overcome the most awful of circumstances. Without her, this would have been just another report of facts surrounding a murder, the ensuing trial and the inevitable incarceration.

CONTENTS

CONTENTS

FOREWORD

Jealousy. Rage. Murder. Injury. Disruption. Abandonment. Incarceration. Accommodation. Patience. Forgiveness. Redemption. In this work by author Paul Hoch, all of the words listed previously figure significantly in the narrative. It reads like a novel, but the events and the people involved are real. The author tells a tale that could happen in any small town in America. This type of story is often familiar to local citizenry if the people involved are from the upper echelons of society. But the people in this narrative are working-class citizens who likely were not known by many of the people in the community, and the struggles of their lives were largely unknown other than by those directly involved. This book brings their difficult circumstances to light. The story and the unfortunate events that continue to follow the two main characters for many years after the initial tragic murder are explored in detail throughout the book. The extensive research done by the author to fully develop the story is impressive. An unusual aspect of this work is that the setting of the story and the times in which it occurred play an important role in the book. The reader, if from Carlisle, will recognize the places and events of the town during the middle of the twentieth century. If not from Carlisle, the reader will come to know the town very well.

Paul Hoch is well known in the town and surrounding community. He has been a successful businessman and has served as a leader in a variety of institutions in the Carlisle area. A native of the area, he has a unique perspective on the events that play out in this narrative. Paul Hoch the writer is also well known, although this is his first "published" work. For two years, he contributed a column to the local newspaper, the *Carlisle Sentinel*. The column, entitled "Walk Around Town," described various places and events in the history of the community. Well received and remembered by the readership, the articles were compiled in 2008 and published by the Cumberland County Historical Society in a single volume entitled *Carlisle History and Lore*. He has also written for the society's annual *Journal*. This work will provide the local community with an opportunity to read Paul's first book-length endeavor. Readers from outside the local area will be introduced to the town, a unique time in twentieth-century history and a rewarding and well-told true story.

The opportunity to read and provide input on an early draft of this book was greatly appreciated. It was a story that I did not know, even after working for eleven years as a librarian at the Cumberland County Historical Society. The unusual aspect of having the town and its familiar locations play a role in the book is intriguing and enlightening. One of the most rewarding parts of the story is the way both main characters are able to rise above the tragedy and bring real meaning to their lives. The use of original photographs of the main characters and of the town from the original time provide significant enhancement to the telling of these events.

DAVID L. SMITH

Editor, *Cumberland County History*, Cumberland County Historical Society
Co-author, *Penn Township, Cumberland County Pennsylvania, 150 Years*
Director, Camp Michaux Recognition and Development

ACKNOWLEDGEMENTS

M y first thanks go to Earl Keller, who started me on this project as a tale of redemption for a family friend, Norman Morrison. He had already completed enough research to pique my interest.

Thanks to the staff at the Hamilton Library of the Cumberland County Historical Society, Cara Curtis, Debbie Miller and especially Beverly Bone, each of whom spent time digging out oftentimes obscure information on everything I asked for; and to Richard Tritt, curator of the CCHS photo archives, for finding the absolutely perfect photos to enhance the readers' experience.

To Randy Watts and his friends John Sheaffer and Dave Houseal, all fire department and East End historians who provided details and linkages for both, often adding color to the story.

To Hannah Cassilly, from The History Press, who helped me all the way through the project.

To Dorene Benjamin, Dolores Davies, Sandy Mader and David Smith, all of whom gave me feedback after reading drafts.

To my friends who never yawned as I told and retold the story.

And lastly and most importantly, to my wife, Lois, for supporting everything I've ever undertaken and for allowing me to get lost in this project for hours at a time.

PREFACE

A couple years ago, a friend of mine, Earl Keller, said that he had a new story for me to write about. I was almost afraid to ask him what it was since I had recently researched and written two other stories from the past that he had suggested. But they had been fun to do and turned out well, so I plunged headfirst into what was going to be the most intensive research I'd ever done. And along the way, I'd get one of the biggest surprises of my life.

In 1926, a twenty-seven-year-old man named Norman Morrison fell in love with a forty-year-old divorcée named Frances Bowermaster McBride. They both lived in the East End of Carlisle, he on a short, one-block-long street named Elm and she on Louther, which was a major street running east–west through the entire town. Both were factory workers, although in two different factories, he at the Frog, Switch and Manufacturing Company and she at the Carlisle Shoe Company. The Carlisle Shoe Company, founded in 1862, was one of three shoe companies operating in Carlisle at the time, making the industry very important to the town. Much earlier, in 1846, when Carlisle had a population of about 4,500 people with six tanneries in operation, there were forty-six shoe "establishments" in the town. By 1926, the industry had consolidated into much larger and more efficient enterprises.

The Frog, Switch and Manufacturing Company was founded in 1898, when it was known as the Manufacturing Company. In 1907, the name was changed to the Frog, Switch and Manufacturing Company to indicate the growing importance of its main products: railway track work. Better

Left: Norman Morrison at about age twenty when he lived on North West Street. *Rupp Collection.*

Below: Interior of the Frog, Switch and Manufacturing Company, circa 1930. *Cumberland County Historical Society, Carlisle, Pennsylvania.*

known to everyone in the town of Carlisle as simply Frog and Switch, it was a noisy, dirty, dangerous place located at the far end of East High Street on the outskirts of town. Inside its corrugated steel walls, once painted yellow but now mostly rust, crews of workmen worked shifts around the clock making heavy railroad products known as frogs, the special section of rail that allowed trains to cross over or switch tracks. Along with the frogs, the crews also made the moveable parts called switches that engaged the frogs. Norman Morrison was a laborer there and had been for several years.

The buildings themselves were several stories high, but since each was designed to provide space for specific parts of the process, they were of varying heights. The resulting impression when viewed from the street was a hodgepodge. In the highest ones were the furnaces, placed there to take advantage of gravity when pouring the molten metal into the casting molds. Smoke, sparks and steam could often be seen. Cranes used to hoist the raw materials screeched along on their own steel rails. It was so noisy that men had to generally shout to be heard. On the coldest winter day, it was hot in the furnace area. In summer, it was nearly unbearable.

In 1926, Norman lived with his mother, Naomi, and her parents. After Naomi gave birth in 1899, at the age of fifteen, to Norman, the two had continued living with her parents, Lewis and Mary Morrison. Lewis was a laborer at Frog and Switch, and they lived in a nice middle-class neighborhood at 445 North West Street for about fourteen years. Then Naomi married George Jacobs and left the Morrison home, moving to Hershey. Sometime between 1922 and 1924, and for unknown reasons, the Morrisons moved from West Street to 154 Elm Street. There, Norman continued to live with his grandparents. Naomi and George Jacobs had recently returned to Carlisle, where George took a position at C.H. Masland & Sons carpet plant. They moved to Kerr Street, where in just a short time, on July 1, 1922, George Jacobs died suddenly at the age of thirty-seven. Naomi then lived on Fairground Avenue for a while. But by 1926, she was living again with her parents and Norman on Elm Street, possibly rejoining the family because of her mother's ill health. Mary Morrison, Norman's grandmother, died in early July 1926, less than one week before the murder to come.

Frances Stuart might have been born in Middletown, Pennsylvania, in 1885. At some point in her early life, her mother, Katherine, married George Bowermaster, and Frances was known in town as Frances Bowermaster, although she legally retained the name Stuart. It shows on her marriage license and death certificate with the notation: "father unknown."

Frances Stuart (Bowermaster), circa 1902, possibly her Carlisle High School senior picture. *Georgia Corvino collection.*

In July 1902, Frances and her newlywed husband, James McBride, moved in with his parents at 342 Mulberry Alley, just around the corner from her mother and stepfather, George and Katherine Bowermaster, who lived at 235 North East Street. James McBride was a laborer in a machine shop, while his father-in-law, George, was a blacksmith's helper at Frog and Switch. Frances and James then moved a couple of times with the two older girls and were at 114 East Louther Street by 1920, next door to where Frances, after her separation from James, had moved with her three-year-old daughter, Georgia, and two older daughters, Mildred, age seventeen, and Helen, age thirteen. This was where Frances was murdered on July 12, 1926. Directly across the street was the Cumberland Fire Company.

After the separation, Norman and Frances had been seeing each other for a year or so and had begun to talk of marriage. But by June 1926, it was obvious to Norman that Frances's ardor was beginning to cool, although he wasn't sure why. As the summer wore on, he began to obsess over the possibility of losing her and actually wrote her several threatening letters, which she would often show to friends and then say, with a smile, that she was still alive.

Finally, on July 12, she handed Norman a note saying that there was no future for them and that she was marrying a soldier from the post and would wear the very same wedding dress Norman had purchased for her. In an almost blind rage, he retrieved a pistol he had recently purchased from his room and made his way to her front steps on Louther Street, where she sat with three-year-old Georgia on her lap. He shot Frances three times, killing her almost instantly. As she fell to the sidewalk, the little girl slid to the side unhurt. Norman then turned the gun on himself and fired. The shot missed him completely. He fired another shot into his right temple that left him unconscious and, later, blind but did not kill him. Little Georgia was taken across the street by a neighbor, and there is no further account of her.

Norman was in the hospital until he could be judged fit to stand for a hearing. A grand jury indicted him for the crime of murder, and he was sent to a state hospital for the insane for evaluation. After three years and a directive mix-up, he was sent back to Cumberland County to stand trial for the crime. He was found guilty and sentenced to life in prison.

Although an atheist at the time of the murder, after a few years in prison, he developed a strong Christian faith and began to assist the prison chaplain. He applied in 1939 for a pardon, which was granted, and he lived in a home for the blind in Philadelphia for the rest of his life.

All of this information was gleaned from accounts in the *Evening Sentinel*, Carlisle's daily newspaper, courthouse records, letters from Norman to members of the Keller family, longtime friends of Norman Morrison living in Carlisle, Cumberland County Historical Society research and interviews.

However, little Georgia McBride was an enigma. What had happened to her after being taken across the street? During the course of more than two years of research, no evidence or even mention of her was ever found. Where did she live? How was her life? When did she die? So many questions remained unanswered.

In March 2013, Cara Curtis, the librarian at the Cumberland County Historical Society, where much of the research has been done, received the following handwritten letter inquiring about certain features in Carlisle in the 1930s:

To Whom It May Concern,

I'm writing this letter because members of my family want answers to some questions, but I can't remember some of them myself.

I'm from Carlisle, Pa. I was born and raised there. I left when I was 19. Some things were good, some bad.

I was 3 yrs. old when my mother was killed on July 12, 1926. She was 41 yrs. old. She was killed by a man, whose last name was Morrison. She was holding me when he shot her.

I can still think about it and remember all too well that time. I can remember the argument they had when she took me for a walk, and they argued in front of school building. After we came home, we sat on front steps, when it happened.

I had two sisters, Helen and Mildred, 10 and 14 years older than me. They are now both gone. They were married to Army men from the Post. They got to travel to Hawaii and overseas and the USA. I always stayed put.

After that happened, I lived with my grandparents until they died and then with my oldest sister Mildred. When her husband was transferred to Hawaii, they couldn't take me, so she brought me back to Carlisle and gave me to Mike Smith, who she said was my father. He was a fireman for the Cumberland Fire Company (I was five).

Members of my sister's family want some answers about things, so I want to help them.

I'll be married 70 yrs. on April 2nd. My husband was also stationed at Carlisle Barracks. We met at the skating rink across from the entrance to the Army Post.

They want names and places, but some names I forget. We used to come to Carlisle every summer to visit relatives. They are now all gone also.

When we go to Carlisle, we get off on High Street to center square. We turn right (I need name of the main street), go one block, turn right on East Louther Street. There was Texas Lunch on corner at one time. My sister Helen lived on opposite corner on second floor for awhile.

One block down there is a stone building on left corner. There was a bar on first floor at one time. Helen also lived there on the second floor for awhile. *If you turn left, part way up was school on right. I need the name of school. I went there from 1 thru 6 grades.*

If you turn right, part way up my grandmother had a confectionery store. Need name of street.

Go back to Louther Street. Fire Company is on left. Right across was house where my mother was killed. Last time we were up, it's painted gray—with dark gray trim and still only a couple of steps out front.

After this happened, my sister Helen worked in shoe factory. Was there only one? Need name and location.

I lived at 245 E. Louther St. until I was 19.

Go to corner, turn left, and one block over, turn left. Evening Sentinel *newspaper was on right. Are they still there? Name of street. If you turned right, you could go through playground to back entrance to Army Post.*

In late '60s my sisters came to see me, and we went to newspaper office, and that's how I got article on my mother's death and date. I didn't think of it at the time, but could you get me some copies of obituaries of several deaths?

I would like one of my mother, Frances McBride—July 12, 1926.

My grandmother died several months or so after. Her name was Katherine or Catherine Bowermaster. I then lived with my grandfather, and we lived with a family named Hershey on High St. His name was George Bowermaster. Is it possible to get these for me?

I always thought some were buried at Westminster Cemetery, but could never find graves. Who could I contact for that?

When my sisters came to visit me, I hadn't seen Mildred for 40 some years and Helen for 20 some years. They traveled a lot with Army husbands. We had a great visit. When they came back to states, they settled in California, and that's where they died.

About 20 years ago, we were able to take a trip to meet all my nieces and nephews. We had a great time, and we all keep in touch.

When I was small, I could hear whispers about things, and when the man who shot her was in paper years later, I could hear all the whispers. I was curious what kind of man he was and whatever happened to him.

I had nightmares for years. I would see my mother rolling onto the pavement. I was shown the dress I had on, all blood stained. I then put it aside, and years later nieces and nephews wanted information so had to recall it again, but it was OK.

Maybe you can help me with these few questions.
Names of street, shoe factory, obituaries, etc. Would appreciate it very much.

Thanks,
Mrs. Georgia Corvino

Georgia had been found!

The day the letter was received, I called Georgia, and she agreed to talk with me if I went to where she lived, a small town a couple hours north of Carlisle. I didn't know it at the time, but shortly after our conversation, she had called Cara at the historical society to make sure I wasn't some kind of con man. Or worse. Cara assured her that I was OK, and within a couple days, I drove to her house accompanied by my friend Earl. We both were filled with anxiety over what we would find when we rang her doorbell. What we discovered was a delightful lady looking about fifteen years younger than her actual age and her equally pleasant ninety-one-year-old husband. They had celebrated their seventieth wedding anniversary just days before our visit.

Earl and I spent about an hour with them while Georgia told us some of her story. After encouraging her to write down her memories, we said goodbye. Georgia and I wrote a couple notes back and forth, but I still wasn't learning much of any consequence. And then, one day, it came—a manila envelope containing thirty-nine handwritten pages filled with the details of Georgia's life. What a thrill to have her share that much. Everything pertaining to Georgia's personal life has come from those pages. Some information on physical things, such as her schools, the Texas Lunch, et cetera, was garnered through additional research.

In the end, this is a true story about two lives that were dramatically changed because of a murder in Carlisle's East End. Both are inspiring, but it has been most amazing to watch Georgia put up with sorrow, mistreatment and misery while persevering with tremendous character to overcome all of that and create a beautiful life with the soldier she met in a roller rink.

CARLISLE, PENNSYLVANIA

In order to better understand the environment in which this murder and subsequent events occurred, it is important to understand a bit of the history of this former frontier town named for Carlisle, England.

James Letort was born in Philadelphia to Jacques and Anne Letort, French-Swiss Huguenots who had gone to London to escape Catholic persecution and then immigrated to Philadelphia in 1686. Eventually, James and his father became Indian-language interpreters for the colony and, later, traders. When Jacques died in 1702, James continued trading, always moving a bit westward. In 1719, he entered the area that would become Cumberland County and settled with his wife, also named Anne, close to a large Shawnee village near the Great Beaver Pond, later to become known as Bonny Brook. The pond was fed by a clear limestone spring that then made its way about nine miles across the valley in a northeasterly direction to meet the Conodoguinet Creek at what would later be named Middlesex.

On April 1, 1751, the governor of Pennsylvania instructed his agent Thomas Cookson to look over the newly founded Cumberland County—which at that time included everything west of the Susquehanna River north of York County and stretched to beyond the Allegheny Mountains—and recommend a site for a town that would become the county seat. The site was to have an abundance of water that was easy to obtain and access to roads and trails that led over the mountains. After some investigation, Cookson decided the town would be best located beside "Letort's Spring," hereafter referred to as the Letort.

Cookson recruited Nicholas Scull, a surveyor, to assist him in drawing a plan to present to Governor Hamilton. Along with the plan was their narrative that the Letort "provided good water, meadows, pasture, timber, stone, lime and other conveniences necessary for the town." Hamilton approved the site, and Cookson set forth to purchase the several plantations from several settlers among the many Scotch-Irish immigrants who had already begun to settle in the area. This was completed in 1753 with the collection of about 1,500 acres.

Carlisle's East End was the first section of the Pennsylvania frontier town that was settled because of the abundant water supply provided by the Letort, which flowed through it. As white settlers came to the area, they usually stopped beside the water. Tanneries, breweries, distilleries and other industries dependant on water and water power sprang up as more and more people came west from Philadelphia looking for new lives. The first bridge in Cumberland County was a wooden affair built to span the Letort in 1780.

By 1800, quite a few farmers had cleared land in the area, and the demand for leather for clothing, harnesses, buckets and more abounded. The 1840 census shows that six tanneries were operating in Carlisle, all along the west bank of the Letort. And of course, the hardworking men at the tanneries were very thirsty, so there were also six breweries in the vicinity of the Letort.

As the town grew toward the west, many of the more sophisticated residents moved in that direction, leaving behind some of the rougher elements of the town in the industrial section. The East End's reputation stayed with it through the next two centuries, and its people were often referred to as "wharf rats"; in fact, they sometimes wore the appellation with cocky pride. Adding to any innate tensions was the army post, located just northeast of the Letort. The mix of soldiers, hometown girls and local boys was sometimes quick to explode. In mid-March 1863, after an early evening of drinking in various East End taverns, a local rowdy named Charley Foulk shot and killed Corporal Barney, leader of a squad of soldiers assigned to patrol the East End to "keep the peace." Foulk consequently became a sort of folk hero, continuing a life of petty crime until he was shot to death in a poker game in Arkansas. His body was returned to Carlisle and buried in the Old Graveyard.

By 1926, the tanneries were gone, and the Eighteenth Amendment to the Federal Constitution enacted Prohibition across the country. This effectively eliminated the breweries and distilleries from the neighborhood. But factories still claimed the East End as their domain, and much of the earlier rowdiness remained. The town of Carlisle was pretty typical of hundreds of small towns in America. Its residents numbered about twelve thousand, and many of them worked in the many factories spread around the town. There were four carpet mills led by C.H. Masland and Sons, two dress factories, three shoe companies (one of which, the Carlisle Shoe Company at the corner of Bedford and Penn Streets, employed Frances McBride), a foundry and the Frog, Switch and Manufacturing Company, where Norman Morrison worked. Most of this industry was in the East End, while much of the town's intelligentsia and industry leaders had moved to the western side of the town square. Out there were located Dickinson College, the J. Herman Bosler Library and the Dickinson School of Law.

BESSIE'S HOUSE

The two-and-a-half-story gray shingled brothel known as Bessie's House at 20 East Locust Alley was being run by the third generation of the African American Andrews family, having been passed to Bessie Andrews Jones from her mother, Cora Andrews, in 1922 or 1924, depending on which record is accepted. The business itself was probably established by Bessie's grandmother Jane Andrews. The 1860 census listed Jane as twenty-nine years old, born in Maryland, mother of three children and employed as a cook. It is unclear when the whorehouse first opened, but most historians believe it was shortly after the census was taken.

In any case, ownership and management passed into Cora's hands in the late nineteenth century. While there is no record of Jane ever running afoul of the law, Cora nearly made a career out of being arrested. Between 1886 and 1923, she was arrested, tried and convicted ten times on the same charge: keeping a bawdyhouse. Each time, she went to prison for a short time, paid her fine and was released. Finally, at the age of seventy, she passed the business on to her daughter Bessie.

A large, plump woman given to wearing big floppy hats and too much makeup and walking with the aid of a cane, Bessie was known all over town. Most residents overlooked or simply tolerated her business. She spent money in the shops downtown, always paid in cash and was very charitable to black and white people alike. She managed to keep the law at bay for the most part, possibly because her client list was said to include only the better class of citizens—those in positions of power. She allowed no college students or riffraff to enter the establishment. She was known to have two girls working for her who were rotated with two different girls every two weeks.

Bessie would, on occasion, be arrested and hauled into court, but she was always successfully defended and released. Her attorney was Hyman Goldstein, who would be a central figure in the divorce case of Frances McBride and the murder trial of Norman Morrison.

CUMBERLAND FIRE COMPANY

Following a January 1809 house fire in the First Ward (East End) near the Letort that killed two residents and seriously burned a third, the Cumberland Fire Company organized in February in the Black Bear Inn, a public house licensed to Christian Humrich on the northwest corner of Hanover and Louther Streets. The original membership was composed of a group of men known as the Cumberland Bucket Brigade. Their first apparatus, called the Water Witch, was stored in the town hall, which burned down in the arson fire of 1845. For a while after that, their home was on the southwest corner of Bedford Street and Liberty Avenue. Since most of their active members lived in the First Ward, they moved in 1896 to the firehouse location on East Louther Street, almost directly across from where Frances lived in 1926.

The Victorian-style station itself was a three-story brick structure with a stone front on the first level. In the center of the front was a pair of wood and glass doors large enough for horses and equipment to pass through. To either side of that was a narrower door for men to enter. The station was the town's most elaborate firehouse and its tower the most ornate. The thirty- by ninety-foot lot had been purchased for just over $900. An innovation was the hose tower. Typically built in the rear of most stations, this one was in the front, eliminating the need to drag hose the whole length of the building. At the rear was space for a future stable with enough room for three horses. The lighting was gas.

The first horses, John and Joe, a pair of sorrels, came to the Cumberland in 1910. Of the four fire companies in town, three now had horses. They practiced and exercised on the streets of Carlisle every day. Kept in the rear of the station, the horses were trained to respond to the sound of the alarm by finding their places under their harnesses, which hung from the ceiling. They were quickly snapped to the harnesses and made ready to go. After some practice, this response time from alarm to rolling apparatus was

Cumberland Fire Company on East Louther Street, circa 1926. *Cumberland County Historical Society, Carlisle, Pennsylvania.*

reduced to less than thirty seconds. No longer were dozens of men needed to hand-pull the rigs.

Shortly after the horses came on the scene, a new piece of equipment arrived: a chemical engine that had two thirty-five-gallon copper tanks each charged with seventy-two ounces of sulfuric acid, ninety-six ounces of bicarbonate of soda and thirty-five gallons of water. The chemicals, when released, made an effective fire extinguisher—provided the blaze was still in the early stages.

This apparatus required two horses to pull it, two mechanics and two chemical men, one of whom was William Sebelist, who would later testify at the trial of Norman Morrison. The turnover of horses was rather frequent, as the excitement of a fire call often made them temperamental, and late in 1911, two new horses were purchased. The *Carlisle Herald*, in February 1912, ran the following:

> *The Cumberland Fire Company's fine engine horses, Jim and Jeff, showed their lack of exercise and surplus of spirit by plunging right through the large front doors of the engine house this morning. Jim and Jeff are not badly hurt, but there isn't much left of the doors.*

Four years later, a ninety-horsepower motorized engine was purchased with a seven-hundred-gallon-per-minute pump and a sixty-gallon water tank. One of the drivers of this engine in 1926 was Mike Smith, who was the first to call the police station after the shots were fired. He would also provide testimony at the killer's trial. Frances McBride lived directly across the street. Her flirtatious nature might have led to intimacy with him for a brief time, and Mike Smith would land directly in the middle of the life of Frances's daughter Georgia.

JULY 12, 1926: 8:34 P.M.

The pain behind his left eye made him imagine that three drops of blood were trickling down the side of his face. His heart was pounding—so loud that he was sure it could actually be heard nine feet, eight and a half inches away. That was the kind of imagined detail that always gripped Norman. Especially when he was agitated.

What he was not imagining, but what was very real indeed, was the cool, hard four-inch barrel of the .32 Savage automatic pistol he had jammed into his pants pocket before leaving the house he shared with his mother at 154 Elm Street. He had purchased the pistol from his close friend Luther Rupp a few weeks earlier. He had put one bullet in the chamber and made sure the clip was fully loaded with ten more.

He was barely aware of the slight uphill grade as he approached Bedford Street. At the corner, he quickly turned to the left and continued past the Carlisle Shoe Factory, stretching between Elm and Penn Streets. He didn't even glance toward the restaurant on Penn Street where the hill crested and sloped down to North Street.

The pace of his walking on the warm evening was somewhere between quick and forced. Twenty-seven-year-old Norman Morrison was on a mission, one of which he was not even yet fully aware. He didn't pause at North Street but strode right past the stop sign, looking neither right nor left.

The pain got worse as he passed the spot on North Bedford Street that had started all of this. It was in front of the Penn Elementary School in the shade of the tall maple trees that she had told him there was no future for them, that she wouldn't see him again. It was where she had given him the letter, where they had argued.

From there to the corner of Bedford and Louther Streets, it was exactly fifty-seven steps. Steps that, for Norman, were always one-quarter inch shy of a full yard. Always. They had not varied for the last fifteen of his twenty-seven years.

His normal countenance was serious, and now a smile was a lifetime away. His always-dark eyes were even darker. The round glasses he wore made him look a little like a surprised owl. His build was rather average and slim. He always stood ramrod straight, his hair brushed straight back. He had a birthmark on the left side of his face. His hands were those of a factory laborer, having worked the last six years at Frog and Switch.

Even though he had dropped out of school at age fourteen after eighth grade to help provide for his family, he was bright and a voracious reader. He knew, for instance, how many Lucky Strike cigarettes it would take lying end to end to reach from Carlisle, Pennsylvania, to Cleveland, Ohio. Not in a straight line, but on the available roadways. And how many Pall Malls, since they were a different length.

As he turned left and headed east on Louther Street, he saw her. She was sitting on her small porch in front of the brick row house at number 112 with her curly haired three-year-old daughter, Georgia, on her lap in a pink and white sundress. The early July evening was just beginning to cool, although there was not even a whisper of a breeze through the trees that lined both sides of the street. Across the street from her house sat Mike Smith in front of the Cumberland Fire Company, where he was the paid driver.

Morrison maintained his pace—thirty-five and three-quarters inches to the stride. Even when he crossed the street, he didn't vary. When he got to within exactly three and a half feet of her, Norman Morrison pulled the pistol from his pocket and shot the pretty forty-one-year-old Frances McBride three times, killing her almost instantly. As she fell to the sidewalk in a widening pool of blood, little Georgia miraculously survived and was unhurt. No words had been spoken. The pain in his eye was now throbbing in rhythm with his heart—116 beats a minute. Without another thought, he pointed the pistol at his own head and pulled the trigger. He missed. His second shot was better, but instead of killing him, it struck his optic nerve and left him blind and unconscious.

Within minutes, Frances's cousin Pearl Glass, who lived just across the street, swept up the blood-covered little Georgia and carried her over to her house. Mike Smith called the police department from the phone just inside the firehouse. James McBride rushed from the poolroom of Rueben Swartz at the corner of Bedford and Louther Streets to his ex-wife's side. People began to gather, and chaos set in.

2

GEORGIA McBRIDE: REMEMBERED OR NOT?

Years later, Georgia thought she could remember her mother arguing with a man in front of the school and then, taking Georgia by the hand, walking home and sitting on the front step. Then, a little later, there was a bright flash and a loud noise, and she fell from her mother's lap. And she had a picture in her mind of her mother rolling off the steps and into the street side gutter. And then she remembered nothing after that.

But she was always haunted by the question of whether it was a valid memory or someone had simply told her about it. After all, she knew research showed that memories formed by children as young as three almost always faded by the age of ten or twelve. On the other hand, the trauma associated with this tragedy might well have burned itself into her retrospection.

At any rate, there she was in the Glass kitchen being wiped as clean of her mother's blood as could be managed. And she was crying softly, not really knowing what had just occurred. She was given a cookie, which eased the crying a bit. Pearl took that opportunity to telephone Georgia's sister Mildred, who by that time was recently married to a young army officer, Edward Clark, assigned to Carlisle Barracks. Mildred quickly came to the Glass home and gathered little Georgia into her arms, cookie crumbs and all. Mildred and Ed immediately made room for Georgia in their home, even though they had not had much time to become accustomed to being married.

Georgia's grandparents George and Kathryn Bowermaster realized that the arrangement was not the best for either Georgia or Mildred and

Frances with daughter Georgia, circa 1923. *Georgia Corvino collection.*

Ed and decided to take little Georgia to live with them. The house they rented at 216 East High Street had been the scene of a bloody suicide in the very room that was to be Georgia's. The back wall was still stained with the blood of the poor, unfortunate soul. Along with the blood was another unusual item: a toilet. Georgia spent the next few months of her young life in these strange surroundings.

POLICE ARRIVE

Police chief Ross Trimmer arrived on the bloody scene with Officers Raymond Wolf and Fullerton Speck. In addition to the two people lying on the sidewalk, there was blood everywhere, running from the corner of the house down the gutter and into the street, pooling around the bodies.

The chief, a tall, commanding figure of a man well known in the East End, had to take charge of the rapidly growing crowd that had already gathered there. When he and the officers had moved the mob away from the scene a bit, he commandeered two cars, one belonging to Robert Baker, into which they placed Frances, and the other the car of Richard James, which in turn was loaded with Norman. Off they sped to the Carlisle Hospital.

The hospital was fairly new, having moved from its former location on North West Street to its new home in the Old Mooreland section of town on July 24, 1916. A newspaper account reported, "On the north side alone there are 26 windows and there is not a dark corner throughout the hospital." One thousand people had attended the opening of the three-story limestone sixty-bed facility. Dr. R.M. Shepler, a longtime Carlisle physician, was president of the board of trustees.

Wary of contagious diseases, no admittance was allowed for patients suffering from bubonic plague, whooping cough, measles, scarlet fever or smallpox. Charity patients who were judged to be incurable were released. A five-dollar charge was levied for use of the emergency room, and the board was investigating the idea of heating the operating rooms and the

Above: Carlisle Hospital, between Wilson and Parker Streets, circa 1926. *Cumberland County Historical Society, Carlisle, Pennsylvania.*

Left: Dr. R.M. Shepler, circa 1930. *Cumberland County Historical Society, Carlisle, Pennsylvania.*

maternity ward. The horse-drawn ambulance was operated by Urie Lutz, a local undertaker, until May 10, 1927.

Frances was pronounced dead on arrival at the hospital, having been shot in the jugular, the abdomen and the arm. Acting coroner John Boyer requested that undertaker William Ewing take charge of the body and remove it to his funeral parlor, which had been founded by his grandfather. William was the third generation of Ewings to own and operate the funeral business.

Alexander Black Ewing had come to Carlisle from his birthplace in Middletown, Dauphin County, in 1849 at the age of eighteen. Having stayed in school longer than most boys of the time, he was well equipped to make his own way. During his boyhood, he had worked with his father driving mules on the Union Canal towpath. He was too ambitious, however, to allow that work to be his life's own.

When he moved west to Carlisle, he boarded in the household of Jacob Fetter, a cabinetmaker. Also in the 1850 census listing for the household were Jacob's son David and another boarder, Alfred Cree, both of whom were cabinetmakers as well. A.B., as Alexander soon came to be known, apprenticed himself to learn the cabinetmaking trade with Henry Fetter, another of Jacob's sons. As almost all cabinetmakers also doubled as undertakers, he learned that trade as well.

In 1853, he went into business for himself at 159 West High Street and continued there until his death in 1903. When an accident in 1893 left A.B. unable to personally supervise the business, his twenty-seven-year-old son Hastings, who had been working with his father, stepped forward to assume management of the firm. Both father and son took great pride in the quality of their work, and the funeral business thrived.

When Hastings died in 1924, his son William J., who had received his license to practice the art of undertaking in 1920 and had been associated with his father on West High Street, relocated the Ewing Funeral Home to his own home at 148 South Hanover Street.

Meanwhile, at the hospital, Dr. Shepler was attending to Morrison in the emergency room and ascertained that Morrison's second self-inflicted shot had entered the right temple, about a half inch below his brain. He was talking incoherently, leading Chief Trimmer to the conclusion that he would get no information from the wounded man unless his condition improved overnight.

So instead of interrogating Morrison, he assigned a guard detail to prevent escape for as long as the man remained in the hospital. Drawing the assignment were Constables Sylvan Clay for daytime duty and Ardell Butterfield for night

Hyman Goldstein as a football player at Conway Hall prep school, circa 1914. *Cumberland County Historical Society, Carlisle, Pennsylvania.*

responsibility. They were each paid a fee of four dollars a day for the duty.

At least three hundred people had gathered by now in front of Frances's house. Stories swept through the crowd like a windblown brushfire. It was generally known by everyone that the probable cause of the shooting was jealousy. Most residents of the town's East End knew that Morrison had been seeing Frances for some time and had been smitten by her beauty and charms almost from the first time he had seen her. Certainly from the first time she had smiled and spoken to him.

Although her divorce from James McBride was finalized in March, they had been separated for more than three years before that. Frances had filed for divorce on March 10, 1925. Herman Berg Jr., the divorce master, fixed Wednesday, the sixth day of January 1926, as the day for taking testimony; two o'clock in the afternoon as the time; and his office, International Order of Odd Fellows (IOOF) Building, 31 West High Street, as the place. The notice of the meeting was sent by registered mail to

James McBride, and the return receipt was attached to the record. James did not show up, but the meeting started on time. Frances was present and represented by Hyman Goldstein, Esq.

Frances was sworn in, and questioning by Mr. Goldstein began. The transcript follows just as it was recorded:

Q. Mrs. McBride, where do you live?

A. 112 East Louther Street, Carlisle, Pa.

Q. How long have you lived in Carlisle?

A. About twenty-five years or more.

Q. For the past twenty-five years?

A. Yes.

Q. Are you married?

A. Yes indeed.

Q. To whom?

A. James M. McBride.

Q. When were you married?

A. 1902, twenty-four years on the first day of July.

Q. Where were you married?

A. Courthouse, Carlisle, Pa.

Q. By whom?

A. Mr. Bentz [a county official].

Q. Samuel Bentz?

A. Yes sir.

Q. Immediately after your marriage, did you go to housekeeping?

A. No sir, I had to live with his people, or I couldn't have lived with him at all.

Q. Where did you go to from there?

A. On North Street, the first time, we only lived there two months when we broke up and then I went to each of the sisters and around to the mother, and then he made me live in the alley, then we broke up again.

Q. Then where did you go?

A. To his sister on Bedford Street, then to the mother again, then I got a house and we lived on Louther Street going on six years, then from there to East Street, then on Louther Street again, then I had to go to Bedford Street and stay there six months, then back to Louther Street.

Q. Do you have any children to Mr. McBride?

A. Yes sir.

Q. What are their names and ages?

A. Mildred, sixteen, Helen, twelve, and the baby, Georgia Kathryn, two years in August.

Q. What was the conduct of your husband towards you?

A. Not good at all. My life was miserable from the day I married him. When I first married him, I couldn't stay in bed, he knocked me out of bed and I had to sit up all night in a cold room. I would take cold and I would nearly die, I had to be doctoring all the time, the doctor thought I was going into consumption.

Q. Did he support you?

A. He never kept me, I had to write to my people at times at Middletown to get money to live on, he gave me $5.00 a week when I first married him, I had to pay Ed Cronican, pay the rent and insurance and the rest I had to live on.

Q. How did he treat you?

A. He would grab me by the neck and wrist and I had children on my lap. He had all the skin twisted off my wrist.

Q. How often did that occur?

A. Every other day, sometimes every day he would strike me and threaten me that he would cripple me or starve me to death if I would send for my people. He said he would kill my stepfather if he would come in the house. They have been sent for at night to come to my place when he was abusing me so.

Q. You stated that shortly after your marriage he ill-treated you?

A. He didn't give me enough money to live on, he would knock me out of bed and abuse me all the time.

Q. How often did he knock you out of bed?

A. So many times I can't remember how often it was.

Q. He struck you often?

A. Yes.

Q. Did he choke you?

A. Yes.

Q. Made your body black and blue from striking you?

A. Yes, he threw me down across a chair, he was half drunk and he wanted me to dance with him. He used to back me up towards something and then he would knock me down.

Q. Did he ever curse you?

A. Yes.

Q. What did he call you?

A. I was a whore and everything he could think of.

Q. Son of a Bitch?

A. Yes.

Q. Did you work?

A. Yes I worked in the shoe factory until I had children and then I washed and ironed for at least a dozen people in Carlisle and keep the house going. I went to see Mr. Boyer [justice of the peace] and I had him in front of Mr. Boyer.

Q. For what?

A. For his treatment to me.

Q. Mr. Boyer told you what?

A. He told me I was to take the children and go away from him. There was no use of living with him.

Q. And as a result of his ill-treatment towards you were you placed in the care of a physician?

A. Yes.

Q. Did he ever threaten to kill you?

A. Dozens of times.

Q. Did he have the means to kill you?

A. Yes he had a revolver and I took it and hid it. He scared my grandmother pretty near to death, she pretty near died. I hid the revolver and he thought he had left it over in the barber shop and he got another one and he told me he would kill me or starve me to death. I never knew what it was to get any money from him since I was married to buy anything with.

Q. You were compelled to leave him?

A. He told me time and time again what he would do if I didn't leave, that morning I didn't answer him and he said if you are not out of here by dinner time, if you will not go by good talking to you will have to go by other means.

Q. You felt your husband would do you bodily harm if you remained?

A. Yes. He would wait until the children and me would go to bed and he would think they were sleeping and then he would start in to fuss with me. Some of the men over at the engine house would yell at him to shut up, they would say, shut your damn mouth and let that woman sleep. It was impossible to endure it any longer. I lived with him twenty years and I never had enough to eat. I would often send down to my mother to get something to eat for the children and myself.

Q. What was the date you left?

A. January 10th 1923

Q. Have you lived or cohabited with him since that time?

A. No indeed.

Q. Did he have any love for the children?

A. I would say not. He wouldn't take any of them on his lap, he said he didn't want to smell like a married man. If they would bump against him or skin his shoes he would fuss and carry on terrible. He has the first time yet to buy anything for them.

Q. How did you treat your husband?

A. Too good.

Q. Would you prepare his meals for him?

A. Yes indeed I would get things in the house with my own money, he never paid for the things, I never got that much money from him, but he never missed his meals. His clothes were always ready for him. I would have to get his water ready and carry it up stairs for him to take a bath, and he would take a bath, and then I would have to go up and bring the water down.

There the questioning ended, and there was, indeed, no doubt that Frances McBride had been long mistreated by her husband. Although Frances might have exaggerated a little bit and possibly played to a small extent with the facts, nevertheless Master Berg reported to Judge E.M. Biddle Jr. that "in my opinion the grounds alleged in the application for divorce are well founded" and recommended that the divorce decree be granted. Along with his report, he submitted a bill to the court for a master's fee of twenty-five dollars and a stenographer's fee of ten dollars.

During their courtship, which had begun sometime after the separation, Morrison and Frances often spent time walking in Garrison Lane, a short, unpaved street with only two houses that led from East North Street to an entrance to the Carlisle Barracks army post. A few times there in the lane, they even talked about marriage, and most of Frances's friends had heard about that, of course. Morrison was so sure of the coming union that he began to give Frances some money to help with her expenses each time he got paid. In addition, he even bought a wedding dress for her to wear on the big day.

But the big rumor, with more than a grain of truth, racing through the hungry-for-gossip crowd gathered at the murder scene was that the romance had lately cooled off, at least as far as Frances was concerned. The whispers revealed that she had recently been seen in the company of a soldier named Walker from the post.

Shoppers and gossipers outside the market house, circa 1930. *Cumberland County Historical Society, Carlisle, Pennsylvania.*

Finally, about eleven o'clock that night, Chief Trimmer returned to the crime scene and sent everyone home. But of course, the gossip and rumors continued into the wee hours of the morning and, for weeks afterward, wherever a few people were gathered—at clubs, shops, poolrooms, backyard fences and particularly at the market house, a feature in various forms on the southeast corner of the square since 1802. The current imposing brick structure was home on market days to 150 vendors and a few hundred shoppers. On Saturdays, the crowds that gathered at the market were there as much for socializing as for shopping, and this corner of the square was a hotbed of gossip. More gossip was exchanged there than over any backyard fence in town. Without a doubt, the murder of Frances McBride was the number one topic being discussed at the market for several weeks in the summer and fall of 1926.

The next day, Morrison's condition was only slightly improved, although he was able to speak off and on. Dr. Shepler had Morrison moved to an operating room and removed the bullet from the left side of his head even though it had entered on the right side. When Morrison regained consciousness, he felt unusually strong and asked a nurse if he might sit. Presumably, she granted his request, although the newspaper account makes no mention of her response. Dr. Shepler said he had a chance for recovery but would not make a positive statement at that time.

4

CORONER'S AND
GRAND JURIES

In the meantime, Constable J. William Smith brought a charge of murder against Morrison before Justice J. Freed Martin. At two thirty in the afternoon of July 13, a coroner's inquest into the death of Frances was held at the W.J. Ewing undertaking establishment.

To the officials gathered that July 1926 afternoon in the funeral home, there was no doubt that Frances had been killed and that all the early evidence pointed to Norman Morrison as the perpetrator. It was decided that a follow-up inquest before a coroner's jury would be held the next day at the courthouse.

Six influential men from town composed the jury, led by Burgess Merill E. Hummel. Testimony was taken from eleven witnesses, some of whom had seen the actual shooting.

Mildred Roney was the first to testify. From her own front steps just two doors away, she had seen Frances sitting on the very bottom step of her small porch. She said she heard no sounds before the first gunshot and clearly remembered the report from the pistol's barrel as Morrison fired the first two shots.

Next to give testimony was Mike Smith, the Cumberland Fire Company engine driver who by that time was very familiar with the threatening letters Morrison had written to Frances. He said that when the first shot was fired, Frances fell off the porch step, and on the third shot, she fell completely to the sidewalk. He identified the shooter as Norman Morrison.

Dr. H.H. Longsdorf was the next witness called. He lived in a large brick house on the eastern end of the village of Centerville, about ten miles southwest of Carlisle on the Walnut Bottom Road. An 1879 graduate of Dickinson College and an 1882 graduate of medical school in Baltimore, he was part of the generation of doctors who would travel to patients both by horse and buggy and, later, by automobile.

His sister Zatae was the first female graduate, in 1877, of Dickinson College, where she had experienced much harassment from the male students. She, like her brother and father, was also a doctor and was one of the first women in Manchester, New Hampshire, to drive an automobile. She also flew her own private plane to the 151st commencement of Dickinson in 1928.

Dr. Longsdorf testified to the findings of the autopsy he had performed on Frances's body. He had found three bullet-entry wounds: one in her neck, which had severed her jugular vein and caused a quick death; one in her right arm; and one in her abdomen.

William Sebelist then testified somewhat cryptically that when he would meet up with Frances on the street occasionally, she would say, referring to at least one threatening letter she had received from Morrison, "Well, I'm still alive. See? A barking dog never bites." He also said that he had seen Morrison talking with Frances in front of the school a short time before the shooting, and Morrison did not seem to be in any way angry. He was, in fact, playing with the three-year-old Georgia.

Following testimony from two or three more witnesses and a visit to the scene of the shooting, the verdict of the jury was that Frances Bowermaster McBride had come to her death by a gunshot wound made by a revolver in the hands of Norman Morrison.

As the next three weeks passed, Morrison continued to improve, although his eyesight did not return. He remained blind in one eye and greatly affected in his other. Finally, at about four o'clock in the afternoon of August 3, he was released from Carlisle Hospital and transported to the Cumberland County Jail by Chief Trimmer, Officer Wolf and Constable Smith.

Resembling a Norman castle with its towers and turrets, the Cumberland County Jail, as it stood in 1926, was completed in 1854. The basic construction was of limestone with a brown sandstone front. The high stone wall along Bedford Street was more than two feet thick at the base and slanted inward to prevent escape. From the alley in the rear, you could peer into the exercise yard. The interior arrangement was a typical two-floor affair with an open center and an iron stairway at one end leading to the upper level. The walls on each level were lined with small cells, each containing two cots, a sink, a toilet, a barred window and a barred door. In addition, there was a

Cumberland County Jail, circa 1929. *Cumberland County Historical Society, Carlisle, Pennsylvania.*

small library, a sick room, a dining hall and a meeting room. This would be Morrison's home until it could be decided what should be done with him.

While in the jail, Morrison was visited by the friends he had developed over the years. One group of those friends consisted of Will Keller; Frank W. Nickel Jr., Will's brother in law; and Acey Brubaker. Beginning about 1920, this bunch had become very close and had taken to walking every Sunday afternoon the roughly seven miles round trip to Waggoner's Gap. Most of the time was spent telling outrageous stories to one another and laughing like fools. Since the trek lasted about three hours, it wasn't too long before Will Keller's wife, Alvah, reminded Will that he had a family at home. So Will dropped out of the Sunday afternoon group but remained close to Norman.

The same day Morrison was returned to the jail from the hospital, Justice Martin said that no date could be fixed for a hearing until Morrison was physically able to attend. If he had mental trouble because of the wound in his temple, he would not undergo a trial. If found otherwise, he would stand trial unless a guilty plea was entered.

A grand jury had been empanelled, and on Tuesday, September 21, at 9:30 a.m., Sheriff Craighead and Deputy Peffer brought Morrison from the jail to the courthouse—along with Tom Collins, who was being charged with the murder of his sister's common-law husband—to await the finding of the grand jury inquest. Judge E.M. Biddle had appointed as defense counsel thirty-six-year-old Hyman Goldstein, who had opened his law practice in

Above: Keller family and friends, 1939: Alvah (left), Morrison (second from right) and Earl (front). *Keller Collection.*

Left: Will Keller (left) and Norman Morrison, 1940. *Keller Collection.*

1920, and J. Freed Martin. Morrison talked only with his counsel and was very quiet. The prosecution was led by District Attorney John E. Myers and F.B. Sellers Jr., Esq., special counsel for the commonwealth, also appointed by the court at Myers's request.

A little before two o'clock in the afternoon, the jury returned to the courtroom, and the foreman, Charles Sayers, reported a true bill in the case. Goldstein moved to continue the case to the December session of the court, saying that "the state of [Morrison's] health is such that he is unable to stand the ordeal of a trial at the present sessions." The motion was granted by Judge Biddle. Morrison was led from the courtroom at 2:00 p.m. and returned to the jail.

5

GEORGIA:
WITH HER GRANDPARENTS

G eorgia was the apple of her grandfather's eye, and she was always by his side, sometimes playing in the large backyard but more often watching cowboy movies in the Orpheum Theater on the north side of the first block of West High Street or at the Strand Theatre around the corner on North Pitt Street. Both theaters were managed by a man named Arthur Glaser, who often made the little girl feel special by making a fuss over her.

The first block of West High Street was the "fun center" of Carlisle in those days. In addition to the Orpheum, there were candy and soda shops with names like the Palace, the Sugar Bowl and the Chocolate Shop. There were also two poolrooms, a drugstore and three restaurants. After the show, Georgia's grandfather would often treat her in one of the sweet shops before heading home.

The Strand was originally opened as the Carlisle Opera House in 1898. An L-shaped affair with dressing rooms to either side of the stage and an orchestra pit in front, it had seating for 1,400 people in three different areas and was heated by steam and illuminated by gas lamps. On opening night, John Philip Sousa's light opera *El Capitan* played to a packed house. Just ten years later, the theater began showing "moving pictures" every evening, in either the main hall or the second-floor assembly hall. At the same time, live performances on stage continued, and Carlisle High School graduations, including that of young Frances Bowermaster, were held there as well. In 1925, the Opera House was renamed the Strand Theatre and was mainly

West High Street, circa 1930. Note the tracks in the street and the arched entrance to the Orpheum. *Cumberland County Historical Society, Carlisle, Pennsylvania.*

used for showing Hollywood films, many of which were of the cowboy genre. The showings were in the main hall, with other areas having been converted to living or storage spaces. Heightening the experience for Georgia was the installation in 1926 of a Robert-Norton theater organ, which triumphantly and without fail announced the arrival of the good guys. During the 1920s, the Strand was advertised as the "Home of Paramount Pictures and High Class Vaudeville."

Grandpa George and Georgia went to those places of fantastic escape so often that Georgia could tell anyone she met the names of every cowboy who was ever in a movie. She especially loved Fred Thomson, number two at the box office in 1926 with *Hands Across the Border* and *The Two-Gun Man*, and Tom Mix, who starred in such silent films as *Tony Runs Wild* and *The Canyon of Light*. But she knew the other eighteen cowboy stars of the silent movies, too.

The theme of those movies fit George's tastes well, as he and his brother had a country and western band, one playing the banjo and the other the fiddle. Georgia's grandmother, Kathryn, demonstrated her musical talent by operating a dance hall, home to many square dances with George both playing and calling the figures. And Kathryn taught all of her granddaughters to dance, even little Georgia.

Poster for a film showing at the Orpheum, 1926. *Cumberland County Historical Society, Carlisle, Pennsylvania.*

Not too long after taking in Georgia, the Bowermasters moved from East High Street to 335 East Louther Street. In the basement of the house, Kathryn operated a small confectionery store, a veritable paradise for little Georgia, the place where she developed a life-long love of Hershey's caramel ice cream. It was in this house, too, that Kathryn died. Georgia stood by and watched as some grunting and groaning men carried her grandmother's heavy, sheet-covered body down the stairs. It was another death that caused disruption in the life of the little girl, now just four years old.

6

NORMAN:
HARRISBURG STATE HOSPITAL

A commission on lunacy examined Norman in the jail on October 7, and as a result, he was committed to the Fairview State Hospital on November 29. Since a new Hospital for the Criminally Insane had been opened at Fairview in Wayne County, in the extreme northeastern county of the state, in 1913, it was an appropriate place for him to be sent for observation and evaluation. For an unknown reason, Fairview was not able to receive him immediately, and he was sent to the Harrisburg State Hospital, formerly the Pennsylvania State Lunatic Hospital. It was established in 1845, and the name was changed in 1921. On December 2, Morrison was placed in the violent ward as a criminal to await transfer to Fairview.

The three-story brick ward building with a small white cupola on the top opened in 1906 and housed the most disturbed and noisy patients. While there was a courtyard and plenty of windows to provide light and fresh air, there were bars and grates on all the windows, doors and gateways, and it was pretty gloomy inside. Norman had a roommate in the sparse cell-like room; the shower and toilet facilities were in a shared room down the hall.

Morrison was assigned to this ward "not because he was insane, but because he was a criminal," as Dr. E.M. Green, superintendent, would later testify at his trial. The ward was set to the far north of the 130-acre hospital campus, which was ringed by the main buildings to the east, the laundry to the south and the administration buildings to the west. Directly in the center sat the chapel, one of only two buildings that allowed men and women to congregate together. The other was the sun parlor, situated just across the sidewalk. At the time, about two thousand patients lived in the facility, which by then had become almost a city itself with its own utility sources, farmland and administration. Indeed, life in the general population was a community affair. Patients worked at various chores all over the hospital, on its farm and in its shops. But Morrison was confined to the criminal ward and could not avail himself of those activities.

Here Morrison would live while Dr. Green waited for the instructions—which never came—to move him to the state institution at Fairview. During the wait, Morrison pretty much just sat quietly and passed the time in a chair. He had not yet learned to read Braille, so he was left largely with his own thoughts. He did receive evaluations from several doctors who would later testify at his trial. After about three years, when no further instructions were forthcoming from Cumberland County court officials, Dr. Green had no recourse but to have Morrison sent back to Cumberland County to await trial.

7

GEORGIA: MORE CHANGES

After Kathryn's death, the odd pair—grandfather and granddaughter—became even closer and moved into a house at 413 West High Street owned by William and Mary Hershey. It was a little unusual that the Hersheys would take in boarders when they did because they had been married only slightly more than a year. Behind the house were the Pennsylvania Railroad tracks, and when a carnival or circus came to town by train, it disembarked and kept its extra equipment there on a lot near the intersection of Louther and Cherry Streets. These were exciting times for Georgia. In addition to going to cowboy movies, a couple times each year one of the circus groups would come to Carlisle, and the delighted little girl would have new playmates from among the circus families for as long as the show lasted.

In the living room of the house, there were two large, gold-framed pictures hanging on the wall, one of Georgia's mother, Frances, and one of her grandmother, Kathryn. George Bowermaster must have taken the pictures to the Hershey home, as there is no evidence that the Hersheys were related to either George or Georgia, although it was clear from things they said that they had known Frances and her girls fairly well. Across from the wall was a sofa, and Georgia used to sit there for hours pretending her mother and grandmother were talking to her and she with them. Those were some of the most wonderful times she had in the year she lived there.

Young Georgia learned from the Hersheys that Frances had been a good mother. She always had her girls dressed in nice clean clothes, many of which she'd made herself. Frances herself was very stylish and attractive.

When a new trend appeared, she was one of the first to get in line. For instance, women then mostly wore their hair in buns, but as soon as Frances saw in a magazine a picture of a woman with short hair, she cut hers—the first in her neighborhood to do so.

Within a year of moving in with the Hersheys, George Bowermaster died in his sleep. Once more, the now five-year-old Georgia had to gaze at the lifeless body of someone she had loved immensely. Her sister Mildred again came and took her to live with her and Ed. By this time, though, they had three children of their own and were living on an army post in Maryland.

The house was part of a barracks-like structure. It had a raised front porch with steps leading up the front. Although she had cousins in the house, Georgia was so lonely that she spent hours alone under the porch with the only toy she had, one she had made from a clothespin and a rag, pretending it was a doll. The loneliness continued for a time, and there was nothing the little girl could do to feel better. The days and weeks and months just seemed to run together in a jumble of fogged memories.

Then the day came when Edward Clark was reassigned to Hawaii. He could take his family, of course, but Georgia wasn't officially part of his family. She couldn't go along. The only place she could go was back to Carlisle. So Mildred loaded the girl and her few belongings into the car and headed back to town. When they got to the eastern end of Louther Street, Mildred parked the car and told the confused Georgia to get out. They then walked over to a brick house numbered 245, the left side of a duplex that had a high, peaked roof in the center. It sat back from the street just a bit. Mildred led Georgia up the four steps to the porch, which had a railing on the end and part of the front. The door was to the right of two windows and almost adjacent to the door of the house next door.   Mildred rapped on the door. When it opened, a man Georgia didn't remember ever seeing before stood there with a questioning look.

Without any small talk, Mildred quickly explained that her family was moving to Hawaii and that Georgia could not go with them. "I've heard the talk about you and my mother," Mildred said. "Now she's yours."

Turning to Georgia, Mildred said, "This is your father." With that, Mildred turned and left, without so much as a backward glance. Georgia was confused. She had never had a father, as far as she knew. What was going on here? The man in front of her in the doorway did not even look like a nice man.

"Get in here," Mike Smith, the Cumberland Fire Company engine driver, said. The door closed behind her with the most frightening sound she had ever heard. What was becoming of her?

Mike Smith with his wife Emma, circa 1935. *Georgia Corvino collection.*

Mike had earlier, in 1901, married Ella Sowers, and the 1910 census shows them living in a rented house at 153 North East Street with no children. It also shows that the marriage was Ella's second. Mike's occupation is listed as house painter. After his divorce from Ella, he lived for a while with his brother John at 247 East Louther Street.

By the time Georgia arrived, Emma Daugherty had moved with her daughter, Gladys, into the house next door to John and was now Mike's second wife. They had recently married, after Mike had lived with her for several years, although the later 1930 census noted that he was a "boarder" in her house. Emma was a heavyset woman with the disposition of a stone. Not sour. Not sweet. Not anything. She came into the front room and looked quizzically back and forth between Mike and Georgia.

"What's this?" she asked. Mike did some shuffling and tried to explain that this little girl might be his. Emma's eyes darkened a bit, but she simply turned and walked away without another word. Nor did she ever speak to Georgia in any sort of loving way or hold her, even when the little girl would cry.

Upstairs were three bedrooms, and Mike took Georgia and the few clothes Mildred had brought with them to the room at the back of the house. Emma's daughter slept in the front room; Mike and Emma shared the middle room. Again, Georgia found herself in the room with the only toilet in the house, so she was warned to turn the other way when anyone used the toilet while she was in bed.

From the very first day in the Smith house, five-year-old Georgia was put to work. Every evening, she had to wash the dishes, and when any of the others found a dirty dish, she had to wash them all again. She scrubbed the kitchen floor. She swept the front porch and sidewalk. She dusted. Often, her stepmother would find some fault with her efforts, and the whole chore would have to be done again.

When she dusted, for instance, she had to pick things up to clear the dust on the surface of a table or shelf. Sometimes she didn't put the object back in exactly the same place. When that happened, Emma would make a big show out of having to correct the mistake. And she nearly always checked the dusting with her finger. If she indeed found dust, Georgia would have to start all over.

The stress of all the work, the trauma of experiencing the deaths of three people she had loved and the lack of love or even a friend in her life now were too much for her to handle. She began to have nightmares and wet the bed. Both these situations simply brought on more discipline and stress. She was so lonely and never felt love from anyone. No one ever held her, and she really had no one to talk to. Consequently, she kept all of her thoughts inside.

NORMAN: TRIAL

The early winter of 1929 was very cold and windy. In fact, November 2 had been the coldest day on record in nearly forty years. The annual Thanksgiving Day football game between high school archrivals Carlisle and Mechanicsburg had been played on a frozen field, with Carlisle eventually winning the game 7–0.

Running the length of the center of High Street were the tracks of the Cumberland Valley Railroad (CVRR), a line stretching from Harrisburg to Chambersburg since its inaugural run on August 19, 1837. Passengers would arrive from either direction and disembark directly in front of the Victorian-style passenger station that graced the northwest corner of Pitt and High Streets, with the Argonne Hotel on the opposite side of High Street.

Among those passengers on December 1, 1929, were several reporters coming to Carlisle from Harrisburg to the east and as far away as Altoona to the west. They would be in town to cover the Morrison trial, which promised to provide plenty of juicy gossip and catchy headlines. Murder trials of rejected lovers always did.

The scene as passengers got off the trains was always one of chaotic confusion. "Baggage smashers" anticipated the arrival of the train and hauled their high-wheeled, noisy handcarts out into the street and near the tracks, where the baggage car would be unloaded. The steam engines huffed and puffed as they approached the station, steel wheels screeched on steel rails as brakes were applied and couplings banged together so loudly that one might have thought they were coming apart. When the train stopped moving and passengers began to alight, a new chorus of shouts assaulted the

CVRR station, circa 1929. Note the baggage cart and tracks in the street.
Cumberland County Historical Society, Carlisle, Pennsylvania.

ears of everyone on the block. Taxi and jitney drivers were calling out loudly to sell their services of transport to one of the many hotels in town.

Because the train sat between the station and the Argonne Hotel across the street, passengers could not easily see the hotel as they disembarked. There was a loud effort made, usually by a young boy sent over from the Argonne, to get the attention of passengers before it was too late and they went to the competition. And get their attention he did—the Argonne was nearly always filled. There were many reasons for its popularity with travelers, but for the reporters, it was because they knew that was where the court sequestered and fed juries, particularly in murder trials. Besides, it was just one block west of the courtroom, and in that kind of frigid weather, it certainly seemed like the best choice.

The amenities the Argonne offered the reporters, as well as other guests, were many. It was arguably one of the finest hotels in Carlisle, its closest competitor being the Molly Pitcher Hotel, two blocks away. The four-story, brick Argonne stood on property once owned by James Wilson, a signer of the Declaration of Independence.

Guest rooms and offices were on the third and fourth floors, reachable by an elevator or stairs, and ranged in price from $1.25 for a single with public bath to $4.50 for a double with running water and private bath.

Argonne Hotel, circa 1929. The lobby entrance is at center, Wertz Cut-Rate is to the left and the coffee shop is to the right. *Cumberland County Historical Society, Carlisle, Pennsylvania.*

A banquet room and office filled the second floor, and retail shops and a coffee shop were on the street level. Here in the coffee shop, where dinner was seventy-five cents, the reporters gathered when court was recessed, hoping to catch snippets of conversations from jurors as they entered and ate their meals.

One block to the east, commanding the square, was the courthouse. The first Cumberland County Court in Carlisle was held on July 23, 1751, in a temporary log building erected for that purpose on the northeast corner of the square. Although temporary, the structure served as the home of the court until a fine brick structure, complete with clock tower, was built in 1765 on the square's southwest corner. In 1820, an annex was erected with room on the first floor to house Carlisle's fire apparatus. But an arsonist set fire to the building on March 24, 1845, after first tying the firefighting equipment so as to render it useless. As a result, the entire courthouse was completely consumed. Almost immediately, plans were made for a replacement. One year and one month later, the new courthouse was finished, costing $49,000 and using more than one million bricks.

In 1929, four sandstone steps led from the front and two sides of the portico to the heavy front door at the rear. The roof of the portico was supported by four tall, imposing sandstone pillars, some of which bore the scars of the Confederate shelling of the town on June 31, 1863. Rising from the front section to a height of 106 feet was a cupola with large lighted clock faces on all four sides, visible from almost anywhere in town.

Cumberland Corner Courthouse, circa 1929. *Cumberland County Historical Society, Carlisle, Pennsylvania.*

Inside, the fireproof walls led to vaulted ceilings, and the floors were red clay tile. Everywhere was a reminder of another time: ornately carved wooden counters, old hanging lamps and heavy doors. Leading to the courtroom on the second floor were two stairways just inside the front door. To the left, the stairs led to the courtroom and on to the clock tower. The stairs to the right led to the grand jury room and then to the courtroom.

Inside the cavernous oval-shaped courtroom was a large pew-like seating section with capacity for about 250 spectators. The benches were arranged with aisles on the outsides, as well as a quarter of the way in from each side. The center section did not have an aisle; rather, a solid divider ran down the middle. All of the pews were painted white with black trim. This section was separated from the front of the courtroom by a sturdy turned wooden railing about thirty inches high.

The light tan walls rose about sixteen feet to meet the white ceiling, with deep multilayered crown molding. The ceiling had sculptured areas decorated with gold leaf. Hanging from it were three heavy chandeliers purchased in 1880. Two of them were in the rear of the room over the spectator section, and each held six lights in a single tier. The front chandelier hung in front of the judge's bench and held ten lights in the lower tier and four in the upper tier.

Around the entire room hung portraits of all the judges who had served. On the back wall was a very large painting of the county seal, above which hung a large clock with a dark face and brass Roman numerals. In each of the front corners were large wood-burning fireplaces with mantels about fifty inches off the floor and heavy iron grates about thirty inches wide. On each side of the room were three tall nine-over-nine windows looking out on the First Presbyterian Church to the north side and on the Kronenberg's men's store to the south side.

Dividing the attorney's area from the judge's bench was a very heavy forty-inch-high wooden railing matching in style that in front of the spectators' section but with curved ends. Between the railing and the bench were the desks for the court clerk and the stenographer. The leather-topped, dark wood–paneled bench was on a raised platform under a porte-cochère supported by twin pillars. The bench served as a desk of sorts, with two wide shelves underneath to the left of the judge's cane chair and two drawers to the right. To one side, a door opened into the judge's chambers, and on the other side, a mirror image of that door opened into the jury room. On the judge's right was the American flag, and on his left was the Cumberland County flag.

In the jury box, to the left of the judge's bench, were twelve swivel-backed chairs, each with a number. The box itself was surrounded by an iron railing about two feet high. The witness stand was also to the judge's left, surrounded by the same dark wood railing but not as heavy as the others. There were two steps up into the stand, and the floor showed the scars of leg shackles dragging across it. The witness chair was made of wood with straight arms and a curved back and was fastened securely to the floor.

On the south side of the building, below street level but accessible from the alley, were the men's and ladies' comfort stations. These restrooms were open around the clock but were especially busy on market days, as the large market house stood on the southeast corner of the square.

In this setting, Judge Edward MacFunn Biddle Jr. would call to order the court that would try Norman Morrison for the murder of Frances McBride. The trial was expected to be brief and devoid of any sensationalism.

On December 2, sixty-three-year-old Judge Biddle made his way from his stone home at 42 West Pomfret Street about a block and a half around the corner to the courthouse. Admitted to the Cumberland County Bar in 1889, he was always a stately and impressive figure, a large man usually clad in a three-piece gray herringbone suit with a neatly folded three-point handkerchief in his breast pocket, covered by his judge's black robe when presiding at the bench. His short brown hair was parted in the middle and looked slicked to his head, and his round face with round glasses could take on the sternest countenance imaginable when his patience was tested.

Judge Biddle called for the Morrison case a little early because two preceding cases had been settled out of court and a third was delayed because of illness. Morrison was brought into the courtroom—a little late because of the unexpected time change—by Sheriff Craighead. The accused appeared interested in all that was going on and raised his head and glanced in the indicated direction of each prospective juror as he was told.

Leading the prosecution was District Attorney Fred Reese, who had been elected to the position after the time of the murder three years earlier. He would later, in 1931, be elected judge in the Court of Common Pleas. He had petitioned the court for the assistance of sixty-seven-year-old William A. Kramer, who had been educated at Dickinson College and was himself a widely known and respected Cumberland County district attorney from 1899 to 1902. Kramer's fee was set at $400. He had prosecuted many homicide cases during his term and had a great reputation as a trial lawyer. He was a dynamic speaker and a good friend and mentor of Reese. Together they had plenty of time to prepare the case against Morrison, which seemed to be almost open and shut.

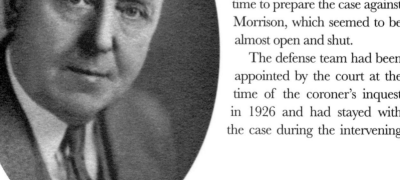

The defense team had been appointed by the court at the time of the coroner's inquest in 1926 and had stayed with the case during the intervening

Judge E.M. Biddle, circa 1930. *Cumberland County Historical Society, Carlisle, Pennsylvania.*

three years. It also had sufficient time to prepare a defense. The first defender was Hyman Goldstein, son of a Russian immigrant and a 165-pound, athletic-looking young man who had opened his law office in 1920. While an undergraduate at Dickinson College, Goldstein, as quarterback, had led the Red Devils to a stunning defeat of Penn State. Both Pop Warner and Jim Thorpe from the famous football teams of the Carlisle Indian Industrial School had called him the cleverest quarterback they had ever faced. Goldstein lived with his young wife, Bertha, at 22 North Hanover Street and kept his office at 31 West High Street. His associate in this trial was J. Freed Martin.

At 10:20 a.m., jury selection got underway. There were eighty-two names in the jury pool. During the examinations, forty were rejected—over half because of opposition to capital punishment. This was

Top: Fred Reese, district attorney at the Morrison trial, circa 1932. *Cumberland County Historical Society, Carlisle, Pennsylvania.*

Right: William A. Kramer, circa 1930. *Cumberland County Historical Society, Carlisle, Pennsylvania.*

Defense team Hyman Goldstein (right) and J. Freed Martin, circa 1929. *Cumberland County Historical Society, Carlisle, Pennsylvania.*

important because it was known that the state would seek a first-degree murder verdict, which could carry with it the death sentence. By 2:30 p.m., five jurors had been selected. They were Mrs. Elizabeth Grissinger, a housewife from North Middleton Township; George Hurst, a clerk from Mechanicsburg; Mrs. Anna Kelly, a housewife from Shippensburg; Samuel Coover, a merchant from Shippensburg; and A.Z. Keck, a farmer from West Pennsboro Township.

Examinations continued, and three more jurors were selected: George W. Morrison (no relation to the accused), a produce dealer from Carlisle; W.A. Leppard, a bank teller from Carlisle; and Lee Gillough, a well driller from Lower Frankford Township. But by then, the original panel had been exhausted. The judge ordered Sheriff Craighead to summon an additional fifty prospects for the next day and recessed the court. A snowstorm that night made travel difficult. Since most of the new panel lived outside of Carlisle, many were summoned by telephone rather than by the customary knock on the door.

Again, more than half were rejected, but with an early start, jury selection was completed by 11:30 a.m. The final four jurors were Frank Zeigler, a farmer from Monroe Township; John Walters, a railroader from Mechanicsburg; Mrs. William Swartz, a housewife from Newville; and

Parker Gillough, a farmer from Lower Frankford Township. Judge Biddle then recessed court until the next day.

In his opening address, Assistant District Attorney Kramer spoke for seventeen minutes, assuring the jury that the prosecution would prove premeditation, as evidenced by the purchase of a revolver from one Luther Rupp, which gun was shown to the jury. He also mentioned a note that Frances had given to Morrison on the evening of the murder, breaking off their relationship and saying that she would not marry him.

The prosecution then began its case. Its witnesses included Dr. H.H. Longsdorf, who had performed the autopsy on Frances's body and gave a detailed description of the woman's wounds. Three bullets had entered her body, one piercing her neck killing her, another striking her elbow and the third hitting her abdominal area.

Chief Trimmer testified that while he was in the hospital, Morrison appeared to fake irrationality every time the chief went there to question him. Rupp was called to identify the Savage .32 automatic revolver found at the murder scene as the one he had sold to Morrison a couple weeks prior to the shooting. He said that it was similar, but he couldn't be sure. Mrs. Albert Kelly lived across the street from the McBride home. She gave a detailed description of the actual shooting. Several other witnesses followed.

In their opening statement, the defense attorneys made it clear that they would be presenting a defense of temporary insanity brought on by a combination of the defendant's unfortunate affair with an unfaithful divorcée, a blow on the head he had received at work two months prior to the shooting, a disease he had contracted in 1917 and the death of his grandmother, who was living with Morrison and his mother on Elm Street, just a week before the awful killing.

Much of the defense's case came from two of the state's witnesses, Mrs. Pauline Kost Howdershelt and Mrs. Julia Steigleman. First, Mrs. Howdershelt testified for the state that she was sitting with Frances when Morrison approached. When she stated that he had walked "very erect and rigid" and that he was "dark, crazy and weird looking," Goldstein sprang to his feet, nearly shouting at the witness, "How did he look?" Goldstein, in fact, got Mrs. Howdershelt to repeat the description several times until finally the judge sustained the state's objection. There was such a stir in the crowded courtroom that court attendants had to repeatedly rap for order.

Goldstein then asked the witness to step down out of the box and demonstrate how Morrison had walked as he approached the women, which she did in a very stiff fashion. Back in the box, Mrs. Howdershelt then testified that Frances had telephoned Morrison earlier on the evening of the murder and asked him to meet her in front of the Penn Elementary School on Bedford Street. Mrs. Howdershelt had accompanied Frances and her daughter, Georgia, to the meeting about a half hour before the killing. While there, she saw Frances hand Morrison a letter, which he put into his pocket unopened. At that point, she said that he appeared "alright." Following the meeting, she walked with Frances and the child back to the McBride home and sat with them on the small front porch. Within a half hour or so, she saw Morrison come walking east on Louther Street. When he was two or three feet away from Frances, he opened fire without a word. After the first shot, Mrs. Howdershelt ran away and knew nothing else of what happened.

She had been on the stand for thirty minutes, much longer than any of the other nineteen witnesses the state had called on the first day of the trial.

The defense scored again with another of the state's witnesses, Mrs. Julia Steigleman. She testified that on the evening of Monday, July 12, she had been visiting her friend and neighbor Naomi Jacobs. During her visit, Mrs. Steigleman had seen Morrison twice. When she arrived at about eight o'clock, he was in a room reading. Although he had dropped out of school at age fourteen—a common practice, particularly in the North Side, where he was then living—to help support his grandparents, he was an avid reader on a broad range of subjects. He had looked up, smiled and nodded a greeting.

About ten minutes later, he went out, seemingly "happy and in good spirits." After no more than twenty minutes, he returned home and entered the kitchen where his mother and Mrs. Steigleman were in conversation. This time, he looked "crazy." His eyes were big and dark, and he appeared very nervous, fumbling with his hair and clothing. He refused to speak to anyone, even when directly addressed. After pacing across the small kitchen a couple times, he went into his room, then came out and left the house.

About an hour before the crime, Wilbur Sebelist had been talking with Frances about his wife, who worked alongside Frances at the Carlisle Shoe Company and was ill. During the trial, he testified that Frances had no fear of Morrison and certainly was not anticipating the tragic event that occurred. He had witnessed the meeting at the Penn School, and between that time and the shooting, he told Frances he had been surprised to see them talking. "I thought you were through with him," he said.

"I am," she replied. "I have just left him, and he knows the reason why." Then she said, according to Sebelist, that Morrison was "crazy, but I'm not afraid of him."

Later in the proceedings, the state produced a letter allegedly written by Morrison and sent to Frances several weeks prior to the murder. Although the contents were not revealed, it was supposed to contain a threat against her life, and it was said that she had given the letter to Justice of the Peace John L. Boyer, who later turned it over to Chief Trimmer.

Another state's witness, Mrs. Albert Kelly, gave a detailed description of the actual shooting. She said that evening she was sitting on her porch at 111 East Louther Street, directly across from the McBride house. Morrison pulled the revolver and fired three shots into McBride, who fell from the porch to the pavement. He then stepped back a pace or two and pointed the gun at his own head, firing two more shots. The first missed, but the second entered his right temple.

The prosecution then began the questioning of Morrison himself. It was revealed that he gave Frances ten to twenty dollars each week to help defray her household expenses and to purchase furniture to be used when they went into housekeeping together. He also gave her money to buy a wedding dress. The courtship continued uninterrupted until the day she told him to no longer call on her at her house. He later learned that she was spending time with a soldier and that part of the money had been going to him. "This," he said, "broke my heart, and I lost interest in everything."

He was then asked about the letter Frances had given him at their meeting at the school. He said that he had opened it on the way home and read that she was through with him and was going to marry Walker, the soldier, in the wedding dress Morrison had bought for her. He said that after reading the letter, he became very stiff and rigid and had the sensation of falling into space.

He said that for some time before the shooting he had suffered from hallucinations, one of which he termed "a malignant entity." It frequently arose before him in the image of three figures that seemed to beckon to him. He appeared to be well read, even though he had quit school at age fourteen. He read books on a multitude of subjects and made frequent radio and photography experiments.

Following testimony from former district attorney John E. Myers that Morrison had admitted to him that he'd written several threatening letters to Frances, extracts of such a letter, allegedly written three weeks before the shooting, were read in court by Chief Trimmer:

> *After what you promised me in the lane that night, do you think I can give you up? I can't do it. I have studied this thing out, and I think you belong to me. No matter what has happened, I am going to have you. It may be any time, any place, anywhere. I am ready for any eventuality which may occur. You are mine, and by the gods I mean to have you. I must do what I have decided; there is no retreating now. If you have any reply to make, call me up.*

The lane referenced in the letter was an early entrance to the post called Garrison Lane, where lovers, including Norman Morrison and Frances McBride, often spent time since it was almost abandoned to major traffic by the 1920s.

Carlisle was perfectly positioned at the intersection of Indian Trails and the Letort to become the jumping-off point for everyone who wanted to head west. It was only natural, then, that Colonel John Stanwix of the British army would establish a permanent military presence there in 1757.

For the next several years, military functions moved in and out of the post, the vacancies sometimes leaving it in disrepair. In 1801, the government paid William Penn's heir $664.20 for the twenty-seven acres it had previously been renting. A School of Cavalry Practice was opened in 1838, and the garrison was a central supply center for ordnance, horses, quartermaster supplies and even freshly fitted troops during the Civil War. In late June 1863, Carlisle Barracks was torched on the order of J.E.B. Stuart.

After the Civil War, as army operations moved westward, Carlisle Barracks' function as a supply depot was discontinued in 1871. After eight years of vacancy, Richard Pratt founded the Carlisle Indian Industrial School, hoping to transform Indian boys and girls into "productive American citizens," the most famous, of course, being Jim Thorpe. The Pennsylvania Historical & Museum Commission marker reads, in part, "This school was the model of a nation-wide system of boarding schools intended to assimilate American Indians into mainstream culture. Over 10,000 indigenous children attended the school between 1879 and 1918. Despite idealistic beginnings, the school left a mixed and lasting legacy, creating opportunity for some students and conflicted identities for others." The school operated until 1918.

On September 1 of that same year, General Hospital No. 31 was established. During the two years of its existence, it provided physical, mental and vocational rehabilitation to more than four thousand soldiers returning from service with the American Expeditionary Forces in France. This function then became, in the fall of 1920, the Medical Field Service School. Here a study was started in 1922 to improve the container and contents of the bandage used in war. Although delayed by economic conditions, it finally found fruition in the new version known officially as the Carlisle bandage.

For more than 150 years, soldiers, and even some Indian School students, had made their way into Carlisle's East End looking for some fun and a good time. Usually that meant flirting with the girls—and more when they could manage it. It was this environment that provided the backdrop for Norman's competitor for Frances's hand.

Shortly after Chief Trimmer read Norman's threatening letter to Frances, the state rested its case at 10:25 a.m. on Wednesday, December 4, after calling twenty witnesses.

J. Freed Martin then outlined the defense's case to the jury. It would be shown that Morrison was "insane at the time he shot the one he loved." As Martin spoke to the jury, Morrison's mother wept silently into her handkerchief as she sat beside her son.

The defense team then called James Bowermaster (no relation to Frances), who lived on Factory Street. He was a longtime friend of Morrison's and testified that the two had many extended conversations on scientific matters and that Morrison had always advanced "impossible" ideas. For instance, he believed that light waves traveled in a corkscrew pattern, that thought waves could play a piano and that he could invent a machine to read a book. Bowermaster also said that Morrison had once declared that he was as far above the average man as man was above the ape. He then went on to say that several weeks before the shooting, a change had come over Morrison. Prior to that, he had always been happy and talkative. Later, though, Bowermaster had been unable to get him to talk rationally, and he appeared to be "heart broken and worried."

The second witness of the morning was Clyde Kelly, of 531 North West Street. He said that on the afternoon of the shooting Morrison had said to him, "I'm going mad." Kelly said that at the time he did seem irrational, nervous and depressed.

Testimony then followed from Dr. W. Baird Stuart, who stated that Morrison was suffering "from a splitting blind headache" and was in a "very profound state of nervous depression" the morning of the shooting. When called to the home of the defendant that morning by Naomi, Morrison's mother, Dr. Stuart had found him in bed suffering from nervousness and depression. He left medicine with him to quiet his nerves.

The defense then called Major Herbert W. Taylor, a physician at the Medical Field Service School at Carlisle Barracks. In support of the defense's claim of temporary insanity, he testified that anyone who acted as Morrison was alleged to have acted for several weeks before the shooting must "certainly have been insane" at the time. He then declared that Morrison was unable to distinguish right from wrong at the time of the shooting.

There followed a long and severe cross-examination of Morrison, who was on the witness stand for more than two and a half hours. The state got him to admit that he had written a letter to Frances before the shooting in which he threatened her, but he couldn't remember the contents or the date.

District Attorney Reese and his assistant, Kramer, dwelt at great lengths on obtaining from Morrison just what he had meant by the words in one letter. Over and over, he replied that he did not remember. He did admit that he had purchased a revolver and cartridges sometime prior to the shooting but could recall nothing of the shooting itself.

Despite the long questioning by the defense and a grueling cross-examination by the state, Morrison showed no signs of any nervousness. He answered questions quickly and in a clear, even voice that could be heard throughout the crowded courtroom. He held a white handkerchief throughout the questioning. Because of his blindness, he had to be led to and from the witness stand by his lawyers.

After testifying, he resumed his seat at the defense table beside his mother, a small, frail woman of forty-seven. Born less than two years before Frances McBride, she was the most pathetic figure in the courtroom. While he sat next to his mother during the testimonies, Morrison sometimes listened with interest but often slumped over and put his head in his hands.

The defense then called Dr. Stuart back to the stand. He testified that the judgment of right and wrong might easily be impaired as a result of an illness such as that which had afflicted Morrison prior to the killing. Stuart was followed by Dr. Wilbur H. Norcross, a Dickinson College professor. He testified that a letter Morrison had written to Frances two weeks before the shooting indicated that the author had no "mental continuity" and that the letter's contents were nothing but a "hodgepodge," showing that the writer "had no judgment whatsoever."

The defense rested its case on the second day of the trial at 2:05 p.m. The state then called rebuttal witnesses, beginning with Dr. Longsdorf. When asked to give his opinion of Morrison's mental condition prior to the shooting, he answered that such a man would have been "sane at the time of the shooting and could have distinguished right from wrong." He declared that Morrison had an "exaggerated ego" and that that was the reason for the crime.

The state then called in succession four doctors from the Harrisburg State Hospital. Dr. Charles Dennison declared there was "no outward evidence of insanity" while Morrison was in the hospital. Dr. Howard Corbus, in examination, found no trace of insanity. Dr. E.M. Green, the superintendent, had been subpoenaed with the note, "Bring records of the Morrison case." He testified that Morrison was brought to the hospital on December 2, 1926, and placed in the violent ward, not because he was insane, but because he was a criminal. He said he was supposed to keep Morrison there until he received instructions to move him to the state institution at Fairview. When the instructions never arrived, he finally sent him back to Cumberland

County. Dr. Booth Miller, the last witness to testify, said that he had never noticed traces of insanity in Morrison. All four said that if Morrison were insane at the time of the shooting, he would still show signs.

With that, testimony was over, and the abrupt end caught the defense team by surprise. It asked for a delay, which Judge Biddle denied. And summation started.

At 3:50 p.m., after the last witness had spoken, Hyman Goldstein addressed the jury for more than an hour, ending with the impassioned plea to "send this poor blind man back to his mother." He was overcome by emotion and finished in tears.

At 9:30 a.m. the next day, the third day of the trial, J. Freed Martin traced Morrison's life and his unfortunate love affair with the woman whom, in the end, he had killed. "This man has suffered enough. Set him free. Won't you? Won't you?" he said in a voice choked with emotion.

District Attorney Fred Reese made the prosecution's final address to the jury at 11:30 a.m. He talked for nearly an hour and a half, asking the jury to eliminate all sympathy from its deliberations and to return a verdict calling for the "extreme penalty."

Judge Biddle's charge to the jury lasted an hour and twenty minutes. He said that the jury could return one of four verdicts: murder in the first degree, murder in the second degree, voluntary manslaughter or not guilty. If found guilty of first-degree murder, his sentence would be death in the electric chair or life in prison.

At 1:20 p.m., the trial was over, and the jury was taken to the Argonne Hotel, just one block down West High Street, for lunch. The jurors began their deliberations at 2:30 p.m., and at 4:26 p.m., they indicated that a verdict had been reached. Judge Biddle, the lawyers and the prisoner were quickly summoned.

When all were ready, Stuart Graham, deputy clerk, went through the orderly drill: "Prisoner at the bar, stand up. Look upon the jury. Jury, stand up. Have you agreed upon a verdict?"

The sealed verdict, signed by Elizabeth Grissinger, foreman, was handed to Graham, who handed it to the judge, who opened it, read it and handed it back to Graham to be read aloud.

"The jury finds the defendant guilty of murder in the first degree with a recommendation of life in prison." The trial was over, and the recommended sentence was mandatory for the court to impose.

The jury was polled. Judge Biddle briefly addressed its members: "I congratulate you on the verdict. You can leave here assured that you did your duty with courage and fidelity."

At the first words of the verdict, Morrison turned ashen gray, and his hands flew to his face. Without a sound, he slowly sank to the floor on his knees for a second or two. He was finally helped to his feet by his lawyers. He quickly composed himself, showing no further emotion. His mother, who had been silently weeping through much of the trial, was not present for the verdict. Morrison talked briefly with his lawyers before being led by Sheriff Craighead back to the jail, where he remained until sentencing.

Because of Morrison's unfortunate plight—he was now totally blind (though of his own doing) and was widely supposed insane at the time of the murder and for a period thereafter—the verdict came as a complete surprise to many. Even the court attendants and lawyers on both sides were not fully expecting a first-degree murder verdict.

A ten-day period was granted by the judge in which to file a motion for a new trial. But the defense team did not expect to seek another trial and issued a statement: "The trial was conducted impartially, and while we are keenly disappointed at the verdict we see no reasons at present on which to base a plea for another."

The next day, December 6, the *Evening Sentinel* carried the headline: "Morrison Guilty of Murder in Death of Alleged Sweetheart. Life in 'Pen' Sentence."

Judge Biddle handed down the sentence on December 23, having waited for more than ten days for the defense to change its mind about an appeal. The sentence included "payment of the cost of prosecution and [the convicted to] suffer imprisonment at Eastern State Penitentiary in Philadelphia, at separate or solitary confinement, for the period of his natural life; and stand committed until the sentence is complied with."

Just four days after the sentencing, the crime and ensuing trial had vanished from the pages of the *Evening Sentinel*. Now, the big story on the front page was the butchering of an 864-pound black Poland China hog by George Deitch for S.A. Brownawell of Kerrsville. The hog was too large for the scalding tub and had to be wrapped in blankets with buckets of hot water poured over them to prepare for scraping off the hair.

The production of that hog was so grand that folks thought it might be a record. Included in the bounty were five cans of lard, eleven crocks of pudding from a kettle as full as if four hogs had been butchered, hams so large it was all one man could do to carry them to the cellar and a head that weighed in at sixty-three pounds.

Meanwhile, Sheriff Craighead was preparing to transport Norman Morrison to Eastern State Penitentiary.

9

GEORGIA: STARTS SCHOOL

Finally, it was time for Georgia to start school at Penn Elementary School—the same yellow brick school her mother had attended and that had figured in her death. The whole feeling was somehow tucked away deep in the young girl's psyche. Shortly after the beginning of the school year, a nurse visited her classroom to talk about hygiene issues. Georgia's seat was the last one in the row, and the official look of the nurse's uniform made her a little nervous. Before long, she had to go to the bathroom. She knew that to do that, she had to put her hand up, but she did so very timidly, barely raising her hand above her shoulder. Either no one saw her request or she was ignored. One way or the other, she just couldn't hold it anymore, and she released her bladder all over her seat and onto the floor.

When the kids around her started to giggle, the teacher came back to find out what was going on. When she saw what had happened, she sent Georgia home right away. Since it was near the end of the school day, she told the girl gently that it was OK and that she didn't have to return until the next day. Nevertheless, the little girl was embarrassed to tears. She gathered her dress around her as best she could to conceal its wetness and started the long walk home. She knew she had to walk past the firehouse, where her father was usually sitting outside along with several other men. She began to pray as fervently as a six-year-old can that he wouldn't be out there today and stop her in front of his friends for ridicule.

But as she turned the corner and took her first faltering steps down Louther Street, there he was, sitting in front of the firehouse alone. And he

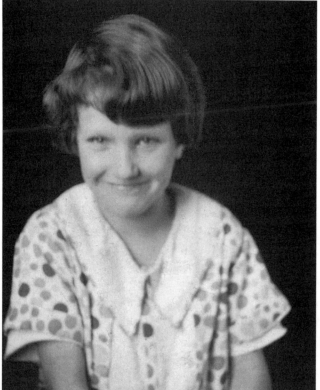

Above: Penn Elementary School, circa 1930. *Cumberland County Historical Society, Carlisle, Pennsylvania.*

Left: Georgia McBride, 1929. *Georgia Corvino collection.*

was watching her all the way. Always afraid of him, Georgia barely looked up as she passed. And Mike Smith returned the cordiality with only a slight nod of his head. As she continued walking east, she began to feel relieved that he hadn't stopped her. She knew that if he had, there was no way she could have hidden the accident from him. But now she was almost home, and maybe she could make her way into her room before anyone else in the house found out what had happened.

No sooner had she closed the front door than she turned and saw her father climbing the front steps. She considered racing up the stairs but knew that trying to escape whatever irrational action he was sure to take was going to be futile. So she just stood there and cried. Mike opened the front door and stared at her.

"So you wet yourself," he sneered. "Take off those wet panties and give them here."

She had no idea what he was going to do, but she knew she had to do as she was told. When she handed him the wet panties, he crudely wrapped them around her head.

"Now get out there on that sidewalk and walk back and forth in front of the house with those on your head. That should teach you a lesson."

Still crying, she again did as she was told. It was then that she experienced the most horrible feeling. Down the street came the kids returning home from school, and coming up the street were the workers from the silk mill at the end of their shift. If she'd had the strength, she would have lifted the grate from the storm sewer in the street and dropped down into it. When Mike was satisfied that enough people had seen her for her to be sufficiently chastised, he called her inside and told her to go up and change her clothes.

10

NORMAN: EASTERN STATE PENITENTIARY

The Pennsylvania state legislature had authorized the construction of the Eastern State Penitentiary near Philadelphia in 1826. Twenty-three sites were originally considered, but a piece of farmland just north of the city in the Fairmount section was finally selected. Because there was a large cherry orchard on the property, the area became widely known as Cherry Hill.

The Western State Penitentiary in Pittsburgh had been authorized five years before, but for many reasons, it was a complete failure and was demolished seven years after it opened. One of those reasons was that the legislative act made no mention of prisoners working, and Western had provided solitary confinement without labor.

By the time the Eastern facility was completed in 1829, lessons had been learned. Individual cells in the new prison were large enough to allow compliance with the new law, passed the same year, requiring inmate labor. The design was that of seven symmetrical cellblock wings laid out as spokes emanating from the center. The perimeter was shaped generally as a circle. From the outside, the structure had a foreboding Gothic castle appearance, presumably to discourage one from living a life that would land him or her behind those awful walls.

Inside, each eight- by twelve-foot cell had a small exercise yard at the rear, although there was not much opportunity for contact among inmates except at mealtime. The dining rooms were long, narrow affairs restricted to specific cellblocks. The meals themselves were pretty simple fare: boiled salted beef,

Eastern State Penitentiary, circa 1930. *Cumberland County Historical Society, Carlisle, Pennsylvania.*

akin to corned beef; Indian mush, a corn meal and water mixture much like polenta; or hamburger with brown gravy and beets. The most popular meal was spaghetti and meatballs. The rotunda was in the center of the prison with a view down each cellblock space through eight-foot arched doorways.

By Morrison's arrival in 1929, one hundred years and a couple of months after the first inmate's entry, many changes had been made to the facility. If he hadn't been blind, he would have seen the large thirty-foot-high limestone walls and the heavy wood and iron admission gate. And he couldn't avail himself of the library containing over ten thousand volumes. Eastern State Penitentiary was not a nice place. And at this point, prisoner #C-5829, Norman Morrison, was not a nice man. Eighteen months after he was admitted, he was described by the chaplain, Fred Smith, as "inclined toward conceit and selfishness, toward none a charitable disposition." Morrison described himself as having experienced "physical suffering and mental anguish [that] have been almost unbearable."

New, too, was the warden, Herbert E. Smith, who came to the prison in 1928. His predecessor, John C. Groome, had been plagued by a series of escape attempts that resulted in more stringent disciplinary policy. Smith continued the "get tough" face of the prison and made wholesale changes

Morrison at a typewriter at the Eastern State Penitentiary. *Keller Collection.*

in the guard staff, replacing many with military veterans. He built sentry boxes on the corner towers and armed the sentries with Krag repeating rifles and Thompson submachine guns. The eight- by twelve-foot cells were large enough but were often cold and damp in winter and unbearably hot in summer. Renovations in the 1930s uncovered an estimated thirty incomplete tunnels.

But Chaplain Smith saw something in Morrison that was worth some effort, and as he worked with him as much as his time would allow, he began to see some softening in the prisoner. Within a couple years, Morrison learned how to type on an ordinary typewriter, how to read and write Braille and how to behave as a model prisoner. He even learned woodworking and built a miniature Ferris wheel similar to the one he remembered at the park in Mount Holly, a doll-sized lawn swing and a doll's dresser, all of which he gave to the Keller family in Carlisle, of whom he was very fond. He was finally reconciled to his blindness, which he accepted not with a trace of bitterness but rather with a sort of cheerfulness.

In addition to escapes, there were a couple other prison life disruptions. In August and September 1933, there was a hunger strike and riot. In November of the same year, there was a mass break for the wall thwarted only when the ladder broke. There is no record of Morrison's participation in either of these events, although at that time he was still "in possession of a selfish self-pitying disposition," according to Chaplain Smith's later recollection.

GEORGIA: APPENDICITIS

Georgia spent a lot of time in her room over the next couple years. She never received anything from her stepmother but disgust and tried to stay out of her way. Dinnertime was especially stressful because no one ever seemed to be interested in her. And if there were something on her plate that she didn't like, Mike would tell her to go to her room without supper. Since it happened fairly often, Georgia suspected that Emma deliberately prepared a side dish or two that she knew the little girl wouldn't like. Mike would never wait too long before he made her try everything in front of him, seemingly just waiting for the opportunity to send her to her room again.

Despite this terrible life in the Smith house, or maybe because of it, Georgia did well in school and was a favorite of students and teachers alike. Homework was an escape for her because no one bothered her, so she spent as much time with her books as she possibly could. When she was eight, she was at the dining room table doing homework when she passed out. She had experienced pain in her right side all day in school, but staying there was better than going home early to face the inevitable questioning about what she had done wrong.

When she woke up, she was in bed and standing at her bedside was a nice man with a black eye patch. He could have been a pirate, but he wasn't. He was a doctor, Dr. Stuart. He was telling her father that her appendix had ruptured and she needed to get to the hospital quickly. While not very compassionate or caring, Mike did manage to take Georgia to the Carlisle Hospital in time to get her into surgery and save the day.

Dr. Stuart, circa 1935. *Cumberland County Historical Society, Carlisle, Pennsylvania.*

According to the medical practices of the early 1930s regarding invasive surgery such as appendectomies, Georgia spent the next two weeks in the hospital being nursed back to strength. Actually, she got more attention and care than she had ever received at home, and unlike most patients, she was not looking forward to being returned to the Smith household. When she did go home, it was with careful instruction to take it easy and not overexert herself. At least she would get a short reprieve from household chores. Of course, that didn't last too long for this young pre-teen.

12

NORMAN : HOUSEMATES

It is interesting to note a few of the most notorious inmates at Eastern State Penitentiary serving time when Morrison was there.

JOE BUZZARD

Perhaps no family had a closer connection to Eastern State than the Buzzards of Pennsylvania's Welsh Mountains. From the late 1800s to the mid-1900s, five brothers (Abe, Ike, Jacob, Martin and Joe) were all imprisoned at Eastern. Joe Buzzard, the youngest of the clan, considered himself one of the premier horse thieves in the country. A remnant of a past era, Joe was the only horse thief in the prison when he entered Eastern for the final time in 1939. There was a time when horse theft was the number one crime at the prison.

ALPHONSE "SCARFACE" CAPONE

Chicago's most famous mob boss spent eight months at Eastern State in 1929 –30. Arrested for carrying a concealed, deadly weapon, this was Capone's first prison sentence. His time in Eastern State was spent in relative luxury.

His cell on the Park Avenue Block had fine furniture, oriental rugs and a cabinet radio.

William Francis Sutton

One of the most famous bank robbers in American history, "Slick" Willie spent eleven years at Eastern State Penitentiary. When once asked by a judge why he robbed banks, Sutton replied, "Because that's where the money is." In 1945, Sutton, along with eleven other prisoners, escaped from Eastern State in an inmate-dug tunnel that went almost one hundred feet underground. Sutton was recaptured just minutes later. Over the course of his criminal career, Sutton was credited with over fifty bank robberies, three successful escapes from prison and more than thirty years served behind bars. He died in 1980.

William "Blackie" Zupkoski

The self-proclaimed "Toughest Man in Philadelphia," Zupkoski was sentenced to from 70 to 140 years at Eastern State for over forty counts of armed robbery. He was apprehended in 1927 following a shootout with police in a local hospital. While at Eastern State, "Blackie" continued his troublemaking ways and frequently found himself in "the Hole" and at odds with his fellow inmates.

13

GEORGIA: SCARLET FEVER

In early February 1933, when Georgia was not quite thirteen, she developed a sore throat that wouldn't seem to go away or get any better. She went to school with it for a couple days, but when it became obvious to her teacher that Georgia was in distress, she was sent home. There she lay on the living room sofa, feeling too bad to even climb the stairs to her room. When Emma Smith came home from her factory shift and saw her there, she immediately said, "Stick out your tongue and lift your shirt."

Georgia had a fine, red, rough-textured rash, a bright red "strawberry" tongue with a whitish coating in the back and the worst sore throat she'd ever experienced. Emma called Mike, who told her to call Dr. Stuart. When he came to the house later that evening, he took one look at Georgia, stuck a thermometer into her mouth, saw the reading of 102 degrees and pronounced the diagnosis, "Scarlet fever."

He immediately announced quarantine. That meant a sign over the front door that banned people from going in or out for thirty days since the disease could be spread both by airborne germs and by contact.

Fortunately for Georgia, an antitoxin had been developed just a few years earlier, and scarlet fever was no longer the death sentence it had once been. Its victims, however, were most uncomfortable for the duration of the quarantine period.

Mike left for the firehouse and stayed there for the duration, which respite Georgia would have relished had she not felt so bad. Emma's daughter, Gladys, moved in with a friend, and Emma stayed to take care of Georgia.

That meant that Emma, in effect, was also isolated for thirty days. She ordered what she needed from Beltzhoover's Food Market on the corner; the goods were delivered and left on the porch. Mike had to check with the grocer about the amount of the bill and then pay it.

When word got to the school regarding Georgia's case of scarlet fever, the whole school had a day off. Her classroom, as well as anywhere else she might have gone, was sprayed, and her books were burned. All the kids had to be checked by a doctor.

Despite the constant stress she had at home, Georgia was very popular in school, and on Valentine's Day, the mailbox at her house was crammed so full of valentines that she almost cried. By this time in history, the lace had been long removed from valentines, and they were made of thicker paper. And they usually displayed a young boy, girl or both with sentiments such as: "Let me take a stab at being your Valentine" and "I'm fishin' for a little girl's love." She was thrilled to get those cards and looked at them so many times that the edges started to curl. The cards and a couple books occupied all her time until the thirty days were up and she could return to school.

When she was in the sixth grade at Penn School, she was chosen to be in the school play for May Day. She was Queen Mighty. A boy named Blake Spahr was King Mighty, and another boy, Richard Wetzel, was Prince Mighty. The memory of the play would later be bittersweet. She loved the acting and was a natural. But the playground where the play was held was just to the side of the Cumberland Firehouse, where Mike Smith sat every day. In all the days of practice and then during actual performance, he never once went around the corner to see her, a fact that would bother her for the rest of her life.

When, as an adolescent, she got her first menstrual period, she was a bit taken aback. She had known from the other girls at school that it was coming, but she still was caught by surprise. In an abrupt turn, it was Mike who told Georgia the facts of life. The talk, though, was laced with implicit threats of what happened to "bad girls." She learned from her stepmother that she had to tear up a sheet to make a belt and pads, and when they were dirty, they had to be soaked in a bucket. When the period was finished, the material had to be washed and laid out on the grass to dry. Through all of that embarrassing time, her cousins next door would tease her without end, and when the stains occasionally came through the back of her dress, other kids laughed at her.

There were several kids in the neighborhood, and they naturally gathered on the corner every evening to play and talk. Most of them had nice clothes; in fact, a different set for each day. But Georgia's circumstances left her often

Georgia as Queen Mighty, Blake Spahr as King Mighty and Richard Wetzel as Prince Mighty, 1934. *Cumberland County Historical Society, Carlisle, Pennsylvania.*

wearing the same clothes for a couple days at a time, and it made her very self-conscious even though none of her friends ever made mention of it. Sometimes the summer activities would go well into the night. At 9:00 p.m., Mike's voice would call out, "Georgia, get in here!"

The whole block heard that call. If she was a couple minutes late opening the door, he would grab her around the neck and shove her inside. The resentment Georgia felt almost consumed her. One night after being roughly pushed indoors yet again, she raised her arm and slung it back so hard that she broke the knob off the door. And of course, she was punished severely. In fact, it seemed to her that she was always being punished. And it was no secret—the whole neighborhood knew how Mike was with her.

During all of her growing up with the Smiths, she never had any toys. She did have board games that she sometimes played with an imaginary friend, making up rules to accommodate the odd arrangement. And she had a device that, with a light bulb and mirror, would reflect a picture onto a piece of paper that she could then trace. Sometimes she spent hours on that—but always alone.

The Harrisburg newspaper had a contest. Anyone who sold twelve subscriptions to the paper would win a doll. She'd never had a doll and just knew she had to sell enough papers to get this one. Since all the neighbors knew what a rough time she was having, the selling was fairly easy. And she got her very first doll. The doll was roughly life-sized, and the winners could choose the hair color and outfits and give the doll a name. It came to Georgia with six round records that could be slipped into a slot in the center of the doll's back. With the aid of the records, the doll counted, said its prayers and sang songs. Georgia was so happy and vowed she would keep that doll forever.

That Christmas, Mike, for some reason, was particularly nice to her and bought her a ukulele. It came with a book, *Learn the Uke in Five Minutes*. In no time at all, she had learned the instrument and was playing songs. In sixth grade, Talent Time was held on Friday afternoons. She got together with a neighborhood girl, and as a duo, they sang and played, and their classmates loved it. She promised herself she would keep that uke the rest of her life. She played it so much that she finally wore out the strings,

When she was thirteen, her family bought her a pair of black slacks and a yellow jersey top. They got her to dress in them right away and took her picture. When the picture was developed and she saw it, she started crying in a big way. She thought the jersey top made her "boobs" stick out in points. To make matters worse, the Smith family laughed and showed the pictures to everyone they could.

Her movements outside the house were very restricted by Mike. She was never allowed to join her friends when they went to Willow Mill Park or to baseball games or anywhere else they went as a group. She remembered going to the movies with her grandfather when she was small and how much she had loved that. Now the only time she could go was Saturday afternoon, and she had to go alone, although she sometimes secretly met one or two of her friends in the dark theater. She particularly loved musicals and often stayed through two showings because she hated the thought of going home.

Sometimes when she would go uptown to the theater, she would see her stepsister, who was also having problems at home, and although they were not close, neither one ever said anything to Mike about what they saw or who they were with.

Georgia's school experience, though, was just the opposite of her home life. She was popular with the other kids. Their willingness to be her friends was almost overwhelming since she never felt that kind of kinship at home. And her grades were always very good through the first six grades at Penn School, then from seventh through ninth at Letort School at the foot of East South Street and even as she started tenth grade at the Lamberton Building, home of Carlisle High School, located on Graham Street about six blocks west of the East End.

14

NORMAN: CLEMENCY

S urprisingly, since he was an atheist before the shooting, in the process of talking with Chaplain Smith, Norman began to develop a deep faith in Christ as his savior, so much so that he acted as an unofficial assistant chaplain, preaching as well as teaching other inmates. Over the next five years, his personality underwent a complete reversal compared to the first five. Neither guards nor prisoners ever had a bad word for him. And on February 14, 1939, he applied to the Commonwealth of Pennsylvania Board of Pardons for a commutation of his life sentence. His application was supported by three letters.

A.G. Fraser, executive secretary of the Pennsylvania Prison Society, wrote that he had known Morrison for the entire time he was incarcerated. He then noted that he had helped develop a plan for Morrison to enter the Pennsylvania Working Home for Blind Men. He expected sponsorship by the Lutheran Bureau "because he is a very devout Lutheran." But if that didn't materialize, the Prison Society would be glad to sponsor him. He went on to say that if the commutation were to be granted, he believed the ends of justice would have been served.

John Meader, superintendent of the Pennsylvania Working Home for Blind Men, wrote that the board of managers had considered the case on two occasions and was willing to accept Morrison to its institution. While the charge for board was four dollars per week, Meader stated that with Morrison's blind pension and the wages he would make in the chair factory, he should be able to get along very well. And Fred Smith, the chaplain, wrote

BOARD OF INNER MISSIONS
of
THE EVANGELICAL LUTHERAN MINISTERIUM OF PENNSYLVANIA
1228 Spruce Street
Philadelphia

February 8, 1939.

The Board Of Pardons
Harrisburg,   Re: Norman Morrison C5829
Pennsylvania.   Eastern State Penitentiary.

Gentlemen:

We understand that your Honorable Body will be called upon
to consider the application for clemency by parole, of this
above mentioned man.

Norman has been known to this organization since January of
1930. The writer began his activities as the Prison Chaplain of
this organization in June of 1931, and has become intimately
acquainted with Norman since that time.

Our observation has been that Norman has made a slow but
steady progress in a revision of his attitude toward society,
and in his entire personality. Formerly inclined toward conceit
and selfishness, toward none a charitable disposition - he has
so completely reversed this personality that today it is prac-
tically impossible to believe that the former personality ever
existed. Today he is one of the finest and most clean-cut young
men of the writer's acquaintance, inside prison or out, and I can
truthfully say that within the past five years I have not heard
any word other than praise for him from either guard or convict.

His has been an honest effort to adjust himself to his present
handicapp of blindness, which condition he accepts with cheerfulness rather than either resignation or bitterness. He has studied
diligently. He is unquestionably a Christian in the full sense
of the word; what more can be said for a man?

I bespeak your sincere and thorough investigation of the
merits in this case.

Respectfully yours,

FAS:MS   Frederick A. Smith (sgd)

Letter from Chaplain Smith to the Pennsylvania Board of Pardons, 1939. *Cumberland County Historical Society, Carlisle, Pennsylvania.*

glowingly in support of the man he said was "unquestionably a Christian in the full sense of the word."

His request for commutation was granted, and he soon moved into the facility at Thirty-sixth Street and Lancaster Avenue in Philadelphia—a free man.

His new four-story brick home covered a city block and consisted of a factory, dormitory and offices. Its purpose was to provide paid employment to blind men who were engaged in the manufacture of brooms, baskets, rugs and chair caning. There was room in the factory for 200 workmen, and the dormitory capacity was 120.

Morrison settled into the routine of a free life as best he could.

Since his religious development in prison had been at the hands of Chaplain Fred Smith, a Lutheran, it was only natural that he would continue that persuasion when he left the prison walls. He became involved with the Church of the Incarnation, an Evangelical Lutheran Church of America. The church traced its history to its first meeting on November 25, 1888, over a meat shop, where twenty-five people were in attendance, but it had moved a couple of times and was now located on South Forty-seventh Street near Cedar Avenue, nearly two miles from where he lived. Even so he was a very regular worshipper there.

Morrison soon began teaching the young people's Sunday school class, was elected a member of the church board and, within a few years, was in demand as a preacher in various churches around the city. He also gave talks on a variety of subjects, but he liked to focus on one of two subjects: the Good News of the Gospel or the situation of blind people in America. By the late 1950s, he was sending sermons to his friends Will and Alvah Keller in Carlisle or to their daughter, Dorcas. These sermons were typically four to six single-spaced typewritten pages with titles that ranged from "Religion and the Public School" to "Did Life Just Happen?" All were scripture based and laced with the warning: "No one will deny that we are in the midst of perilous times."

Even though he would get occasional visits from his Carlisle friends, as a respite from life in the city, Morrison loved to visit Carlisle, usually staying with the Keller family, who lived on North West Street. Generally, he would visit for about two weeks in the summer and again at Christmastime. In addition to staying with the Kellers, he also visited and stayed with the Glenn Burkholder family in the Plainfield area. Glenn's sister, Nellie, was an army nurse and then worked in Philadelphia following the war as a physical therapist. In working with blind men, she became aware of Morrison's Carlisle connection. The children of neither family were aware that Morrison was a convicted murderer.

To get to Carlisle from Philadelphia, Morrison would make his way to the Thirtieth Street train station, where he would board the train bound for Carlisle. Arriving there, he would be met at the station on West Penn Street,

Morrison (right) accepting an award for service to the blind, 1953. *Keller Collection.*

usually by a member of the Keller clan. All the warmth of reunion with friends was evident, and he would then ride with the greeter in a car to the Keller home.

Morrison was known by the family to be kind and compassionate and very gentlemanly. He loved to walk around town and would trust to the end the (usually) young person on whose shoulder he would place his hand for guidance. Often there was a to-do among the Keller girls, all in their teens,

Morrison holding Earl Keller, 1940. *Keller Collection.*

over who would be the one to accompany him. Many times, he would be led to Acey Brubaker's house, also on North West Street, where the two men would have a rollicking time retelling past stories.

Morrison with the Burkholder family, circa 1950. The children are Ronald (twelve), Diane (nine) and Connie (three). *Diane Jumper Collection.*

During his Christmas visits, Morrison loved to go caroling among the neighborhoods. High points of both the summer and winter vacations were his visits to the prisoners in the jail and to the Holiness Christian Church on B Street.

When he stayed with either the Kellers or the Burkholders, he always took them small woven rugs. And he would send the youngsters two or three dollars every year on their birthdays.

15

GEORGIA:
FIFTEEN AND BEYOND

The summer Georgia was fifteen, she felt more alone and hurt than ever. It absolutely seemed as if no one in the world loved her. She couldn't, of course, escape to school to be with her friends, and she was never allowed to go anywhere with them. Sometimes she would go to visit her sister Helen, who lived up the street, but their relationship was never close enough that she was comfortable talking to her about how sad she felt.

Although her stepmother Emma had come from a large family of eighteen children, only four were left in the general area, and they all lived in Harrisburg. They all treated Georgia with more tenderness and warmth than she ever got from the Smiths. Emma's one brother was named Grove and worked as a bartender in various Harrisburg clubs and bars. He kidded Georgia a lot and always called her, for some unknown reason, "Katydid." He always made her laugh.

Aunt Mabel was a widow and owned several beauty salons. She wanted Georgia to quit school and come work for her because she had no children of her own and could teach her the business, but school was the one place where the girl felt she belonged, so she said no to the offer.

Aunt Esther and Uncle Charlie Snoddy came to the Smith house every Sunday. They were nice to Georgia, and she felt warm and comfortable around them. Then one Sunday, out of a clear blue sky, they told Mike that they would take Georgia to live with them in Harrisburg. They rented a house at 427 South Fifteenth Street in a middle-class neighborhood. Mike quickly agreed—what an opportunity to get her out of his life! Maybe the tension constantly running through the house would now disappear. So off they went, Georgia, Aunt Esther and Uncle Charlie. Although Charlie had completed only seven years of school and Esther eight, they were relatively well off. Charlie had joined the Harrisburg Fire Department in 1932 and was an engine driver, wearing badge number 38. He earned more pay than most of the men in his neighborhood.

The day after Georgia's arrival, Aunt Esther took her into the city to shop for clothes—beautiful clothes just like the other girls wore. She had never had so many pretty clothes. "Finally," she thought. "Now I'm with someone who wants me and will love me." She was so happy.

Aunt Esther answered a knock on the door one day and was surprised to see a young man standing there. He said he wanted to see Georgia and asked how she was. Georgia had seen the young man around many times. He would always smile, say hello and ask how she was. Nothing ever went beyond that. She didn't even know his name. And even now, he didn't stand at the door very long after being told Georgia was fine.

But of course, Aunt Esther and Uncle Charlie wanted to know how their niece knew him. For a reason that she never understood, they promptly put her in the car and took her back to Carlisle. Adding insult to injury, Aunt Esther kept all her new clothes. So there she was, back in the clutches of devastating loneliness.

One summer Saturday night, Georgia wanted to go up town and walk around with her friends, stopping in the Chocolate Shop and the Palace, but Mike said no. Many of the neighborhood families were out on their porches enjoying the warm evening. At Mike's refusal, Georgia snapped. "Go to hell!" she shouted as she nearly stumbled down the steps and made her way, in tears, to her sister Helen's apartment in the large stone building on the southwest corner of Louther and East Streets. She stayed there until six thirty the next morning.

At sunrise, she went out and stood on the little bridge over the Letort, wondering what would become of her. The bridge was about two doors down from her house, and she stayed there until her stepmother opened the front door and called her inside. Even with prodding, she never told Mike or Emma where she had spent the night. That refusal set into motion a series of events that would usher in profound changes in her life.

First, a stern-looking man came to the door and took her and the few belongings she had—such as the doll and the uke—to the orphanage on South Hanover Street. She stayed there for several days, waiting for the other shoe to drop. And drop it did. Someone soon showed up and displayed documents that clearly required the fifteen-year-old Georgia to be taken to the Sleighton Farm School for Girls outside Philadelphia.

Her arrival at Sleighton was a scary experience. Her long, naturally wavy hair was cut real short. The physical examinations to which she was subjected were frightening and intrusive. She was heartbroken.

She was given a set of plain clothes and assigned to a roommate. The living quarters were large dorms referred to as cottages, and in each cottage, there were about thirty-six girls. They were all about the same age and had had problems at home, feeling unloved and unwanted. While it was quickly obvious to Georgia that this was a place for bad girls, a sort of reform school, it was also clear that "those girls" were kept in separate cottages in another area.

Each cottage also had a full-time housemother and another woman who covered holidays and weekends. The primary housemother in Georgia's cottage, Harrison, was Mrs. Baldwin, a nice, motherly woman. The 1940 census, taken on April 8, showed that of the forty girls listed on the page with Georgia, she was one of only eight who were educated beyond the eighth grade.

The cottage had certain rules for the girls. They were to be up at a certain time. They had assigned chores. And they were to be in bed at a pre-announced hour. A student council made sure the girls made their beds, showered and did their chores. Any girl who failed to comply came before the council, which would decide what privileges would be taken away. Georgia was immediately accepted at the cottage and quickly became popular. She was elected to the council shortly after her arrival.

In December of her first year at Sleighton, she learned in a letter from her sister that her beloved Orpheum Theater had burned down. The fire had started in the basement of the Peerless Food Store next door, which was owned by the Ryder Dairy of Lemoyne. All that was left of the theater was a small brick portion of the large, arched front entryway. But she also knew that just that summer, a new modern theater, the Comerford, had been built across the street. She looked forward to going to the movies there if she ever went back to Carlisle, but she was enjoying her time at Sleighton too much to think about that very often.

The high school inside the farm was the Martha P. Falconer School for Girls. There, all the girls learned to cook, bake, clean and sew, as well as study the traditional subjects of English, math and science. In the summer, the girls worked in their garden growing their own vegetables. When the cooking class was over, the girls had to cook and serve what they had learned to make. All the girls in that particular class sat at tables around the sides of the dining room. Everyone else sat at a table in the middle of the dining room.

Besides learning domestic skills, Georgia did well in her other classes. She also was involved in the school's athletics, playing softball, soccer and basketball. In addition to all that, she sang in the school choir. She was clearly having the time of her life with no Mike Smith to rein her in.

Every Sunday morning, they all went to church. But on Saturday nights, they gathered in the living room of the cottage and played records and danced. Georgia had made good friends with a girl named Peggy Werner from Lancaster, and they danced a lot together. At the May Day festivity when they were in eleventh grade, they dressed in costumes and danced the tango—Georgia as the man and leader and Peggy as the woman. The rest of the girls at the school loved it.

Georgia did well in art class, and her teacher said she had a gift for it and should pursue it. As a senior, she was part of a group that started a little publication called *Village Chatter*. They all had a hand in writing the articles, but all the artwork was produced by Georgia. She was able to get a job working the switchboard in the school's main building, and she loved it. She went with her class on a field trip to Mount Vernon—a memorable experience. She was indeed having the time of her life.

During that year, she was allowed to go home for occasional weekends, but she put it off for a long time, not wanting to return to that unpleasant situation. Finally, she did go, borrowing a nice dress from one of the other girls. The visit was OK, but not good enough to make her want to do it again. Her stepmother did come to Sleighton once to see her, but Mike never did, which was no surprise to Georgia.

Several occasions during her senior year were very special to Georgia. First, she was elected to be the Virgin Mary in the Living Nativity scene. She and another girl as Joseph sat on the stage in a rough manger with the Baby Jesus. A spotlight shone on them. There were even a lamb and a donkey that were led up the auditorium aisles to be part of the scene.

Then she was elected May Queen. That was a big deal. There were costumed Maypole dances, and everything revolved around the May Queen and her escort. Georgia's music teacher took movies of the festival and showed them to the class. Georgia had never felt so proud and confident. And when she was given her class ring engraved with the name of the school, "Martha P. Falconer School for Girls," she finally felt as if she really belonged to a family.

The real high point, though, was her 1942 graduation. The girls made their own pretty dresses out of white organdy. As they marched into the auditorium singing their school song, each girl was standing a little taller and appearing

Georgia as May Queen at Sleighton School, 1942 *Georgia Corvino collection.*

much more confident than she ever had before entering the school—and most of all, Georgia. As she was handed her diploma, she thought her heart would explode with the sense of pride she was feeling. These were the best three years of her life. She had made many lasting friendships and had learned a host of life's lessons in a warm and loving environment.

But now she had to make an important decision. She could go to live with her older sister Mildred, who by now had six children of her own. She could go to her sister Helen, who had regularly written to her while she was at Sleighton. Helen had even sent her a pretty blue plaid skirt, a blue sweater, a camel blazer and brown and white saddle shoes during her senior year. Or she could go home to the Smith house on East Louther Street. Although she knew what might happen there, in the end she knew she had to go home to be around people who knew her and places that she knew.

Mike had arranged for her to work a job at the Standard Piezo crystal plant when she got home. The name Piezo came from piezoelectricity, whereby an electrical charge is generated in response to applied mechanical stress—in this case, to quartz wafers. The reverse is also true. Thus, when an electrical charge is applied to a quartz crystal wafer, a constant vibration occurs known as "frequency." Various frequencies can be maintained by controlling the thickness of the wafers through a sawing and polishing or lapping process.

The Standard Piezo Company had its origins in a basement room at Dickinson College. In the early 1930s, Dr. W.A. Parlin was a newly arrived physics professor. Three of his students were interested in amateur radio and were encouraged by Parlin to set up W3YC, the college's original radio station.

In their communications with other colleges and ham operators, they learned that quartz crystals could stabilize radio frequencies. They decided to attempt to cut and polish their own crystals instead of buying the more expensive ready-made ones. While they were busy with their radio project, Grover Hunt, a college custodial engineer, was on a family trip to California and brought back some pieces from the Petrified Forest. His intent was to carve a chess set from the material. He enlisted his brother-in-law, P. Reynold Hoffman, to help construct a saw that would cut the extremely hard material. When that proved to be more difficult than anticipated, Hunt became aware of the radio team and decided to try cutting quartz crystal.

Soon, Hunt's knowledge of quartz exceeded that of the rest of the group, and he began to cut entirely rough crystal blanks and sell them to ham operators through an ad in their magazine. Thus began the commercial crystal industry in Carlisle, with Grover Hunt at its forefront.

One of Hunt's largest customers was Linwood Gagne, chief radio engineer for the Goodyear Blimp Company in Akron, Ohio. During a visit to Carlisle in 1935, Gagne and Hunt formed a partnership that resulted in the formation of Standard Piezo. In 1936, the pair purchased a small bungalow with a rear-shed attachment on Cedar Street. But the partners rubbed each other the wrong way, and about a year later, Hunt left the partnership to form his own company.

The industry in Carlisle was fairly small in the early days. Most crystals were sold to ham operators, airlines and the manufacturers of marine equipment. But the approach of World War II changed all of that. Soon, war applications were invented that utilized the crystals, and demand exploded. While there were now four crystal producers in Carlisle, making it the "Crystal Capital of the World," Standard Piezo was the major player and developed many new manufacturing techniques long before they made it into industry publications. To help meet demand, the company moved its operations to East Louther Street and opened a second, larger plant in Scranton, Pennsylvania.

Approximately 95 percent of the company's four hundred production employees in Carlisle were women. They were paid a piece rate so that the higher their personal production, the more money they made. It was fairly common for them to earn $100 a week and even possible to earn $200. Mike told Georgia that from her paycheck, she must pay board, save some and keep the rest for herself.

16

NORMAN: END OF A LIFE

In a letter written to Will and Alvah Keller in September 1959, Morrison indicated that he was beginning to suffer from "leg cramps" and "tummy pains." When not writing of his ailments, however, his tone was generally upbeat. He wrote gratefully, thanking the Kellers for his stay with them that summer. He also recounted giving a speech to the first meeting of the newly formed Club for the Working Blind held at the Penn Sherwood Hotel in Philadelphia. And he was proud of the fact that Mayor Richardson Dilworth and his wife were present to hear him speak.

In a letter written on April 23, 1960, Morrison told Will and Alvah how amazed he was by two new (to him) mechanical devices:

> *We have a machine in our shop that you can put coins in and get out of it bars of candy, soft drinks, hot coffee, etc. It will take coins up to fifty cents and give you back your right change. That machine does a land office business. I heard of a new electronic device for use in banks, etc, that you can put up to five dollars in it and get it changed. The machine can tell the difference between a one, a two, and a five dollar bill, and you can't fool it.*

A little later, in another letter to the Kellers, his typing was fraught with errors as he described his condition:

> *My tummy isn't right, and I feel as if I had neen [sic] hit over the head with awhite [sic] pine board. Hence this mean typing...Please*

overlook this awfuo [sic] *typing. I feel rottenand* [sic] *and can't control my fingers.*

He struggled with his illness for several more months. In his last letter, written on May 21, 1960, to his dear friends the Kellers, he wrote:

Dear Will and Alvah,
This is Saturday afternoon and about half past three. I have just gotten up from an afternoon rest to type a few notes to dear and close friends, and this is one of them.
I have been getting worse all week. I was over at the University Hospital on Friday and was examined for nearly six hours. I have a low bloodcount

Norman M. Morrison

Norman M. Morrison, formerly of Carlisle and a resident of the Pennsylvania Working Home for the Blind, Philadelphia, died on Monday, in the University of Pennsylvania Hospital, Philadelphia. He was 61 years of age.

He was a member of the Church of the Incarnation Philadelphia, and the official board. He was a teacher of the Young Peoples Class of the Sunday School.

Funeral service will be held on Thursday at 10 a.m. in the Church of the Incarnation, 47th and Cedar Ave, Philadelphia with burial in Westminster Cemetery.

Norman Morrison's obituary, June 29, 1960. *Keller Collection.*

and while there is no soreness there are other signs of invalid trouble. I am to be taken into the hospital on Monday morning and if I am lucky I may be out again in six days or so. If I am unlucky..

I cannot eat anything only toast and soup and light foods such as Jello. And it [is] very hard for me to get up and down stairs. I don't think it is my heart, though. It could be anemia or even hemofilia [sic] or some lesser ailment. I am to undergo a series of tests to determine for sure what the trouble is. I am nervous and jumpy and can hardly type. Our Matron's name is Mrs. Helen Riley and anytime you want to contact her about me her address is the same as mine.

Sincerely and with all my love,
Norman

Just a month and six days later, on Monday, June 27, 1960, at 10:00 a.m., Morrison was dead.

17

GEORGIA: NEW LIFE

A nd so her new life began. Georgia was back in her old room with the
toilet in the corner, and somehow that felt comfortable, like renewing
an old and faded friendship. She worked a rotating shift schedule at the
crystal plant, changing each week, on an assembly line preparing crystals for
use in army radios. She loved her job. The pay was good. And things were
looking up for Georgia McBride.

She quickly made friends at work, and when they worked the 10:00 p.m.
to 6:00 a.m. shift, they often stopped for breakfast on the way home from
work. One Sunday, she and a friend took a walk, and both being rather
talkative, before they knew it they found themselves at Black's Roller Rink
on North Hanover Street. The rink had a distinctive exterior appearance
with a large rounded roof reminiscent of a Quonset hut's roof. Neither of
the girls had ever been there before, so they decided to take a look at what
was happening inside.

There were a couple soldiers standing at the soda bar, and they glanced
at the girls. One of them, a good-looking Italian man, focused his eyes on
Georgia's. They smiled at each other, and the girls left. Maybe it was the
organ music, or maybe it was the smile, but right then and there, Georgia
decided to take up roller-skating. She told herself it would be good to
get out of the house, but she also knew that maybe she'd see that good-
looking guy again.

She bought herself a pair of Chicago Rollers, ones that laced up high
and had wooden wheels; they came in a sturdy case with the Chicago Shield

Black's Roller Rink, circa 1942. *Cumberland County Historical Society, Carlisle, Pennsylvania.*

trademark on it. She was at the rink before work, after work and on her days off. One night, Tony, the good-looking Italian soldier, asked her to skate a few times. He was very good on his skates, and she was thrilled that he wanted to skate with her.

On Halloween, she wore a sailor skating outfit that she'd had a neighbor make for her, mostly in the hopes of catching Tony's attention again. She won a prize but wasn't too sure about Tony. Several nights later, though, he asked to walk her home. She was in heaven. But he said to her, "Don't get any ideas. I walk a different girl home every night." She was devastated because she was so crazy about him.

They sometimes met at the Texas Lunch at the corner of Hanover and Louther Streets; there were always several soldiers hanging out there. The popular Texas Lunch was founded in 1925 by Greek immigrants. Its primary menu feature was a hot dog with a snappy skin and loaded with a special and secret type of chili sauce. Showmanship was the key, and people would pause in front of the big window to watch the cook line up hot dogs on

Exterior of Texas Lunch, circa 1938. *Cumberland County Historical Society, Carlisle, Pennsylvania.*

an outstretched arm and apply the sauce, mustard and onions. During one Santa Claus parade in the 1930s, the restaurant sold seven hundred hot dogs in one hour.

Patrons sat in wooden high-backed booths that each had a large number affixed so the waitress could keep the service straight. Although hot dogs were the feature, the menu was complete and offered varied meals at reasonable prices, often followed by the popular pies baked on the premises.

Finally, with a stomach doing flip-flops from nerves, Georgia made herself go in for lunch to see if Tony was there. He came to greet her, and that was it. Georgia and Tony, the love of her life, connected for good. From then on, they were inseparable. They always said goodnight on the bridge over the Letort, which was two doors from her house, because Mike would throw a terrible fit if they kissed on his porch. Sometimes when Tony called on the phone, Mike would answer before Georgia could get there, and he would call Tony a grease ball, a wop, a guinea or whatever other vile name he could think of. He hated everyone who was different from him.

Tony and Georgia dated for about a year under those conditions, and they talked about getting married. During what would turn out to be her last Christmas at home, Georgia asked Mike if Tony could come to the house to pick her up. With a sneer, he said OK. But when Tony came to the door

and entered the living room, he and Mike sat there waiting for Georgia to come downstairs, neither saying more than five words to the other. Mike did notice a wristwatch Tony was wearing and knew that Georgia had given it to him for Christmas. That made him mad, and when Georgia came home later that night, they had a big argument about it. Tony gave her a ring that Christmas. And although it was not a diamond engagement ring, it meant the same to both of them. And she never showed it to Mike because she knew he would be enraged.

They kept talking about how they could get married and finally agreed that the only way Mike would allow it would be for Georgia to get pregnant. With much trepidation, they slept together one time. And waited. One day at work, Georgia got sick and was sent home. The next morning, Mike was filling the parlor heater with coal oil, and the smell of it made her sick. She stayed home again. Her stepmother asked Georgia if she had had sex.

Top: Tony Corvino, circa 1942. *Georgia Corvino collection.*

Left: Georgia McBride, circa 1942. *Georgia Corvino collection.*

"Once"

"You're pregnant."

Those two words, which would have been terrible for other girls to hear, instead made Georgia's heart soar. She couldn't believe her good fortune! Tony called to see how she was, and when she told him she was pregnant, he said, "We're getting married." That night, they decided to get married by a justice of the peace. Georgia moved her stuff out of the Smith house the next day.

Her stepsister, in a rare display of caring, bought Georgia a corsage of red roses. But true to form, Georgia had to meet Tony a block away on the corner. Mike went upstairs and never said goodbye or wished her well. Before that day was over, Tony and Georgia were Mr. and Mrs. Charles (Tony) Corvino.

In the beginning, they lived in a couple bedrooms rented from friends, but within six months, they had moved into a third-floor apartment on East Louther Street, just a few doors down from the Texas Lunch. The curved staircase went from the street level to the top floor.

A 1940s apartment kitchen. *Cumberland County Historical Society, Carlisle, Pennsylvania.*

They had a living room, bathroom and kitchen. In the living room was a sofa bed that they pulled out each night and folded up again in the morning. Also in the living room were a desk, a china closet, a wooden rocker and double windows and doors that led to the fire escape. A pulley line stretched out to a post to hang wash. The kitchen had a gas stove, sink, cupboard, window and icebox. They felt like a real family now and were so happy.

After a couple months, when Georgia was obviously pregnant, Mike got the idea that they should be married in the Catholic Church. The priest at St. Patrick's often stopped by the Smith house to have a couple drinks with Mike, but Georgia never imagined that Mike himself was Catholic, let alone one in good standing. He never went to church, but he did always send Georgia to Mass with a neighbor and her three girls. So Tony and Georgia went to the church and had a talk with the priest, after which he married them in the rectory.

Soon after the "wedding," Tony's eldest and youngest sisters came to Carlisle from the family home to visit the couple. They stayed at the James Wilson Hotel on West High Street and brought along with them a basket full of Italian goodies. They even prepared a wonderful spaghetti dinner for the four of them right in Georgia's kitchen. When they returned home and told Tony's mother how Georgia was carrying the baby, she said it would be a girl. About a month later, Cindy was born at Dunham Army Hospital at Carlisle Barracks.

When Cindy was only a few weeks old, Mike became very ill with a serious prostate problem that required surgery. The day before the scheduled operation, Georgia visited him in the Carlisle Hospital. He told her he needed blood and asked if Tony would be a donor. Georgia was surprised that he would ask such a thing, but she went to Tony with the request, and he said that of course he would. And he was a type match, so his blood was used directly with Mike.

The day of the operation, January 25, 1944, they waited for some word from the doctor, and when the hospital finally called, the news came that Mike had died at age sixty-seven. Tony always joked that it was that good Italian blood that killed him. The visitation was at the Lutz Funeral Home, and the funeral service was held in St. Patrick Church. Burial was at Westminster Cemetery. According to his obituary in the *Evening Sentinel*, Mike Smith had been a driver at the Cumberland Fire Company for twenty-five years, and prior to that, he had been a painter at the Carlisle Indian Industrial School. He had held every office in the fire company and had been reelected vice-president just a week before he died.

When Georgia saw Mike in his casket, it was the first time in her life she had seen him being still, and it felt a little weird. But he was out of her life now forever. His obituary listed Georgia as a "foster daughter." She was twenty-three, and Tony was twenty-four.

Georgia and Tony both doted on baby Cindy. So that Georgia's long hair wouldn't be in the way when she was caring for Cindy, her aunt Mabel gave her a very stylish short cut. When the baby was four months old, Tony told Georgia that he was going to be sent to Fort Lewis in Washington, then to Fort Bragg and then overseas as the war was in full swing. He wanted to take Georgia and Cindy to be near his family while he was gone. So off they went and, in fact, moved in with Tony's parents until Georgia could find a place of her own.

She got the warmest welcome she could ever have imagined. The Corvinos lived in an Italian neighborhood, and the whole place took her in with open arms. She had never in her life felt so loved and wanted by so many people. Her mother-in-law, through her heavy accent, taught Georgia how to cook Italian dishes, and when she did find her own place, the Corvinos had her and Cindy back every Sunday and on holidays for family dinner.

Tony was allowed to go home for a few days before he was to be shipped overseas. The day he sailed, Georgia found out she was pregnant with their second baby. She found a nice apartment in the center of town that was perfect for her and Cindy, although she had to share a bathroom with another couple who lived on the second floor with her. Both they and her first-floor landlord were very good to her, and she was happy.

Meanwhile, Tony was stationed on Tinian Island in the Marianas and was an active part of the war effort; he almost lost two fingers in an accident unloading things from the ship *Indianapolis*. That ship was later sunk, and many men lost their lives. Tony and his unit knew that the plan was for them to invade Japan sometime in the next few days. Before that time came, Colonel Tibbets had lifted off from the island's airfield to drop the bomb on Hiroshima. Shortly thereafter, the war was over, and by late December, Tony and Georgia were reunited.

It was the beginning of a new and wonderful life for Georgia, one that had nearly been snuffed out at the age of three, but one that would welcome another baby, a son, and would last more than seventy happily married years with Tony, the love of her life. Together they produced a son and a daughter, four grandchildren, nine great-grandchildren and two great-great-grandchildren.

Georgia and Tony Corvino at their seventieth wedding anniversary, 2013. *Georgia Corvino collection.*

WALK WITH ME

I f you were able to actually walk the streets of Carlisle's East End, you might more fully understand the lives of the people in this story. We'll start at the beginning, and as you walk, try to imagine how each of the different people in the story might have felt.

THE CRIME

Let's start at 154 Elm Street, the home of Norman Morrison in 1926. In his enraged state, he exited the front door with the pistol in his pocket, turned abruptly to his left and started up the slight rise of Elm Street. Imagine the warm July evening, about 8:30 p.m. Walk with him and remember his quick and measured pace.

At the corner, turn purposefully to your left onto North Bedford Street. As you continue, notice the red brick townhouse on your left. That's where the Carlisle Shoe Company factory was located and where Frances McBride worked.

Continue across East Penn Street, making your way toward North Street directly ahead. Imagine the throbbing pain behind Morrison's left eye brought on by the fury caused by Frances's rejection. But he was too focused to do anything other than look straight ahead.

As you approach North Street, look at the limestone church on the southwest corner. In 1926, the building exterior was brick, with the stone façade being added much later. As Morrison passed, again without looking left or right, the First United Evangelical Church was undergoing its second expansion in thirty years.

Carefully cross North Street and continue on toward Locust Avenue. Pause there for a minute and look to your right. About halfway up the alley on the left side was Bessie's House. The site is now a paved parking lot. Now cross the alley. You will soon come to the Penn School apartments. That is the school building where all the "wharf rats" of the early twentieth century attended elementary school. That is where little Georgia McBride started her formal education and where she completed six grades. And it's where Morrison's pain that evening reached an unbearable level.

When you get to the corner, turn left. Stay on the north side of the street until you are at the end of the apartment property. Now imagine you are Morrison and you see Frances across the street, sitting on the step of the first unit of the light-colored brick house with her toddler, Georgia, on her lap. She is talking with another woman, and you can even hear a faint laugh. Cross Louther Street and stride directly toward her.

When you get to within three or four feet, conjure up the vision of Morrison pulling the pistol from his pants pocket and firing three shots into Frances's body. He watched in horror as she fell to the sidewalk and little Georgia tumbled off, covered with her mother's blood. Knowing he had just done something horrible, although experiencing no remorse, he pointed the pistol at his own head and pulled the trigger. Realizing he had missed, he adjusted the angle of the barrel and fired again, falling to the sidewalk unconscious.

OTHER PEOPLE AND PLACES IN THE EAST END

Directly opposite the murder scene stands the building that was, in 1926, the Cumberland Fire Company. Here Mike Smith was the driver, and he sat, in good weather, outside the firehouse, waiting for a call. He was fifty at the time of the murder.

If you retrace your steps just a bit back to Bedford Street, the red brick building on the southeast corner is where James McBride was shooting pool in the poolroom of Reuben Swartz when he heard the shots. From here, he ran down the street to find Frances already dead.

Now continue east on Louther Street. At number 114, next door to the "murder house," Frances and James lived with their daughters Mildred, ten, and Helen, six, in 1920. About in the middle of the block, on the south side, you'll notice a low, small house with a raised porch. That is one of the oldest houses in Carlisle. You might even be able to see evidence of the logs with which it was built.

A little bit farther is the dark brick house, number 158, where James and Frances lived in 1910 with their infant daughter Mildred. You will soon come to East Street. You are now very close to water, the Letort, and you can really see the character of some of the older houses.

After you cross East Street, you will come to the bridge over the Letort. This is the water that encouraged people to settle here. It is the water, also, that supplied tanneries, breweries, distilleries and any other industry that depended on a good water supply. On the north side of the street, the second house from the stream is number 245, the left-hand side of a duplex. That is the house Georgia McBride entered when she was five years old and where she spent ten very unpleasant years of her life.

If you want to continue, go to South Spring Garden Street, turn left and proceed to North Street. Turn right and you'll find Garrison Lane to your left, directly across from a vacant parking lot.

If you're interested in Frog, Switch and Manufacturing, you'll find that at the end of East High Street, where it changes names to become Trindle Road. The company is the large industrial site on your left.

I hope you've enjoyed the tour of the East End, the relatively small area where much of this story of murder, misery and marvelous perseverance transpired.

CHANGES IN THE LANDSCAPE

If you're interested in learning more about some of the scenes of this book, the following will help in locating certain specific places in Carlisle. Most have morphed into something different or disappeared altogether. Here are the landmarks as of 2014.

THE ARGONNE HOTEL

This building still stands on the southwest corner of Pitt and High Streets. The name was changed in 1938 to the James Wilson Hotel, which operated until the 1950s. It is now the home of Safe Harbour, a nonprofit providing services for the homeless and potentially homeless. For more, see http://carlislehistory.dickinson.edu.

BLACK'S ROLLER RINK

This building still stands on North Hanover Street, easily identified by its rounded roof. It is now occupied by commercial businesses.

CARLISLE BARRACKS

The site of the Carlisle Indian Industrial School and the Medical Field Service School mentioned in this book, the barracks have been the home of the U.S. Army War College since 1951. For more, see http://en.wikipedia.org/wiki/Carlisle_Barracks.

CARLISLE HOSPITAL

The 1926 building was razed, and upscale homes have been built on that block bounded by South, Parker, Walnut and Wilson Streets.

CARLISLE SHOE COMPANY

The property at the corner of Bedford and Penn Streets has been redeveloped into apartments. No other shoe companies remain in town. For more, see: http://wiki.dickinson.edu/index.php/Dianna_Coscette.

C.H. MASLAND AND SONS CARPET MILL

This property on the north side of Spring Road has been razed, and the area will be redeveloped into residential, retail, restaurants and lodging. None of the other carpet mills remain. For more, see www.masland.org.

THE COURTHOUSE

This is now referred to as the "Old" Courthouse and still stands on the square. The courtroom is on the second floor and is open to visitors if no hearings or other proceedings are in session.

CUMBERLAND COUNTY JAIL

This structure is still standing on East High Street and now houses county offices. For more, see: www.visitcumberlandvalley.com.

CUMBERLAND FIRE COMPANY

In 2009, all of Carlisle's fire companies save one, the Union, merged into one department. The Cumberland Fire House still stands on the north side of the 100 block of East Louther Street but is vacant. Pearl Glass's home site is now a part of the vacant lot to the west of the former Cumberland Fire House. For more, see http://carlislehistory.dickinson.edu.

THE CUMBERLAND VALLEY RAILROAD

Neither this company nor any of its buildings or equipment exists today. The station on the northwest corner of Pitt and High Streets was razed in 1941, and the stones were used to construct an apartment building on the southwest corner of South and Parker Streets. JFC, a temporary help agency, now occupies the station's corner. For more, see http://en.wikipedia.org/wiki/Cumberland_Valley_Railroad.

EASTERN STATE PENITENTIARY

This Philadelphia facility closed in 1971 but is still open for tours and special events. For more, see www.easternstate.org.

EWING FUNERAL HOME

This South Hanover Street location is now the home of the Carlisle House, a bed-and-breakfast. The funeral business still operates at 630 South Hanover Street as Ewing Brothers Funeral Home, owned and operated by a fourth-generation Ewing. The current building once housed the orphanage where Georgia spent a few days before being taken to the Sleighton Farm School for Girls. For more, see www.since1853.com.

42 WEST POMFRET STREET

Judge Biddle's home is now the home of Raudabaugh's Barbershop.

413 WEST HIGH STREET

The Hershey home is no longer standing. The property is now owned by Dickinson College.

427 SOUTH FIFTEENTH STREET, HARRISBURG

While this home of Georgia's aunt Esther and uncle Charlie is still standing, the neighborhood is blighted, with many properties being boarded up.

FROG, SWITCH AND MANUFACTURING COMPANY

This enterprise still exists at the end of East High Street. The name has persisted to the present, even though track work has been replaced by large manganese castings for the rock-crushing industry. For more, see www.frogswitch.com.

HARRISBURG STATE HOSPITAL

The Cameron Street facility closed in 2006, and most of the buildings now house various state agencies. For more, see: http://hsh.thomas-industriesinc.com.

THE MARKET HOUSE

This was condemned in the late 1940s as being unsafe and was razed in 1952. A new courthouse now stands in its place on the southeast corner of the square. For more, see www.farmersonthesquare.com.

115 EAST LOUTHER STREET

Pearl Glass's home site is now part of the empty space to the west of the former Cumberland Fire House.

154 ELM STREET

Norman Morrison's home is still a private residence.

112 EAST LOUTHER STREET

Frances McBride's home is still a private residence.

ORPHEUM THEATER

This building burned down in 1939, and the space is now used for parking for the Cumberland County Historical Society. A small part of the curved brick entrance is still visible on the east side.

PENN ELEMENTARY SCHOOL

This building still stands on North Bedford Street and is the home of Penn School Apartments.

PENNSYLVANIA WORKING HOME FOR BLIND MEN

This facility closed in 1979 following bankruptcy proceedings. The building at the corner of Thirty-sixth Street and Lancaster Avenue in Philadelphia still stands and has been converted into apartments. For more, see http://en.wikipedia.org/wiki/Associated_Services_for_the_Blind.

639 NORTH EAST STREET

The home of Mildred and Edward Clark is still a private residence.

SLEIGHTON FARM SCHOOL FOR GIRLS

This Philadelphia institution closed in 2001 for financial reasons. It has been sold to Toll Brothers, which proposes a development of four hundred homes. For more, see http://abandonedsteve.com.

STANDARD PIEZO

This business is closed, as are all other quartz crystal plants in Carlisle, once the "Crystal Capital of the World." For more, see http://www.tedlind.net.

ST. PATRICK CATHOLIC CHURCH

This church where Georgia and Tony were married for the second time still stands on East Pomfret Street. It is now known as the "shrine church," as a new modern church is located on Marsh Drive. For more, see www.saintpatrickchurch.org.

STRAND THEATER

This structure on North Pitt Street burned down in 1972, and an addition to the Cumberland County Historical Society was built on the space.

TEXAS LUNCH

This building on the corner of Hanover and Louther Streets is still a restaurant and bar, although the name has changed to the North Hanover Grille. For more, see www.northhanovergrille.com.

31 WEST HIGH STREET

The office of Hyman Goldstein is now part of a building owned by the Cumberland County Historical Society. The former Odd Fellows Hall is on the third floor.

335 EAST LOUTHER STREET

The home of George and Kate Bowermaster and Georgia McBride for a short time is now a private residence.

22 NORTH HANOVER STREET

The upstairs apartment of Hyman and Bertha Goldstein is now part of a commercial building.

245 EAST LOUTHER STREET

The Mike Smith home, also Georgia's home for about ten years, is still standing and is a private residence.

216 EAST HIGH STREET

The home where George and Kate Bowermaster took Georgia to live is now an abandoned gas station lot on the southeast corner of High and East Streets.

BIBLIOGRAPHY AND OTHER SOURCES

INTRODUCTION

Carlisle City Directories
Cumberland County Historical Society Archives
Hoch, Paul D. *Carlisle History and Lore. Its People, Places and Stories.* Carlisle, PA: Cumberland County Historical Society, 2003.
Watts, Randy, personal interview. December 15, 2013.
Wikipedia. "Cumberland Valley Railroad." http://en.wikipedia.org/wiki/Cumberland_Valley_Railroad.

JULY 12, 1926: 8:34 P.M.

Evening Sentinel, July 13, 1926.
Keller, Earl, personal interview. March 20, 2011.

GEORGIA MCBRIDE: REMEMBERED OR NOT?

Corvino, Georgia, personal interview. April 10, 2013.
———, written account. 2013.

POLICE ARRIVE

Cumberland County Historical Society Archives
Evening Sentinel, July 13, 1926.

Coroner's and Grand Juries

Dickinson College Archives
Evening Sentinel, July 14, 1926.
Keller, Earl, personal interview. March 20, 2011.

Georgia: With Her Grandparents

Corvino, Georgia, personal interview. April 10, 2013.
————, written account. 2013.

Norman: Harrisburg State Hospital

"City on the Hill." http://hsh.thomas-industriesinc.com.
Evening Sentinel, December 5, 1929.

Georgia: More Changes

Corvino, Georgia, personal interview. April 10, 2013.
————, written account. 2013.

Norman: Trial

Cumberland County Historical Society, 2003.
Evening Sentinel, December 4, 5, 6 and 7, 1929.
Hoch, Paul D. "Carlisle History and Lore. Its People, Places and Stories."
    Carlisle, PA.

Georgia: Starts School

Corvino, Georgia, personal interview. April 10, 2013.
————, written account. 2013.

Norman: Eastern State Penitentiary

"Eastern State Penitentiary, Crucible of Good Intentions." 1994 Philadelphia
    Museum of Art.
Keller, Earl, personal interview. March 20, 2013.
Wikipedia. "Eastern State Penitentiary." en.wikipedia.org/wiki/Eastern_
    State_Penitentiary.
www.easternstate.org

GEORGIA: APPENDICITIS

Corvino, Georgia, written account. 2013.

NORMAN: HOUSEMATES

"Eastern State Penitentiary, Crucible of Good Intentions." 1994 Philadelphia
   Museum of Art.
Wikipedia. "Eastern State Penitentiary." en.wikipedia.org/wiki/Eastern_
   State_Penitentiary.
www.easternstate.org

GEORGIA: SCARLET FEVER

Corvino, Georgia, written account. 2013.

NORMAN: CLEMENCY

Application for Clemency. Commonwealth of Pennsylvania, Board of
   Pardons, 1939.
Cumberland County Archives
Jumper, Diane, personal interview. October 24, 2011.
Keller family, personal interview. December 1, 2011.

GEORGIA: FIFTEEN AND BEYOND

Abondoned Steve. "Sleighton Farm School." abandonedsteve.com/
   sleighton-farm-school-3.
Corvino, Georgia, personal interview. April 10, 2013.
————, written account. 2013.
https://www.facebook.com/SleightonFarms
Shaeffer, John, personal interview. December 14, 2013.
Unknown Historic Sites. "Sleighton Farms School." unknowhistoricsites.
   blogspot.com/2012/04/sleighton-farms-school.html.
Watts, Randy, personal interview. December 14, 2013.

NORMAN: END OF A LIFE

Morrison, Norman, letters. 1959–1960.
Philadelphia Inquirer, June 29, 1960.

GEORGIA: NEW LIFE

Corvino, Georgia, personal interview. April 10, 2013.

————, written account. 2013.

ABOUT THE AUTHOR

Paul D. Hoch is a lifelong resident of Pennsylvania, having lived in Carlisle from age four to twenty-two. A career stint with JCPenney took him to points both east and west in the state, but he returned to Carlisle in 1974 and began a career with Hershey Foods Corporation in 1977, from which he retired. He's had a longtime interest in both local history and writing, although this book is his first formally published effort.

Courtesy of Jenn Quigley, Carlisle, Pennsylvania.

He is an active volunteer in various nonprofit groups and is currently president of the board of trustees of the Cumberland County Historical Society. He is also a folk art wood carver in the Pennsylvania German tradition.

He and his wife, Lois, have been married for fifty-five years, live in Carlisle and have three children and five grandchildren.